Understanding the Scriptures

Ethics & Christianity

Luke 24:45

"Then opened he their understanding, that they might understand the scriptures"

By
Stephen R. Hogan

Understanding the Scriptures Ethics & Christianity

4th Revised Edition

Copyright 2007 by Stephen Hogan through CIPO, registration number 1045721: All rights reserved. No part of this publication may be reproduced, stored in a retrieval system, or transmitted, in any form or by any means, electronic, mechanical, photocopying, recording, or otherwise, without the prior permission of the author.

1st Publication March 2012
2nd Publication April 2012
3rd Publication May 2014

Visit www.ltapostolic.org to order copies of this book and to contact the author.

ISBN 978-0-9739282-4-2

Unless noted Scriptural references are from the King James Version of the Bible, also, references are at the end of each chapter and highlighted words are the author's and not from the Bible.

Editors: Michael Valentino & Pastor Efa Brillant Efon

Layout & Cover Design: Stephen R. Hogan

Acknowledgments

I want to acknowledge the contributions of the following individuals to the final publishing of this book.

Mr. Michael Valentino

Michael Valentino, the first editor of the manuscript, helped me to refine this project and pointed out various flaws to improve the content. He helped me to elaborate on important points that were not sufficiently developed. He also reviewed and revised the content more than once. His efforts and constructive feedback was a tremendous asset to the development of this book.

Pastor Efa Brillant Efon (Missionary of the Gospel)

Pastor Brillant, the second editor, helped develop the Scriptural content of this book. Although he focused on correcting the manuscript, his contribution was that of imparting his pastoral knowledge. I appreciate his professionalism, constructive feedback, and spiritual counsel.

Arondowele Agard

My wife wrote the forward, but most of all she supported my efforts and often challenged my writings. Her feedback, questions, and comments helped develop the content of this book. I am thankful for everything she has done.

In short, I would like to acknowledge everyone who helped me work on this book. This book exists because of God and the tremendous devotion made by these people. Without their help, the completion of this book would have been quite difficult. Your efforts are appreciated.

Foreword

Stephen Hogan is a true man of God. He has been told often in times past that God has called him to a peculiar ministry. His unique gift for reaching out to the lost is just one of the many qualities that God has used to build his ministry. His devotion to the work of God within the church and community reflects his willingness to respond to God's call. This book is a perfect representation of this response. Over the past couple of years, Stephen has received revelations from God that have led him to conduct several studies on different topics in the Scripture to compile this inspirational work. In spite of oppositions and obstacles, God opened many beautiful and unexpected doors for this book to be edited, designed and published. This is indeed a real work of God and has blessed the author with spiritual growth and maturity.

Arondowele Agard

Table of Contents

Introduction 1

Section One: The Importance of Spirituality 2

Chapter One: A Spiritual Foundation 3

Chapter Two: Applying God's Standard 8

Chapter Three: Ministries 22

Section Two: Traditions 29

Chapter Four: Law or Grace 30

Chapter Five: Rituals 37

Chapter Six: Holidays 40

Section Three: The Importance of Life 47

Chapter Seven: Against Nature 48

Chapter Eight: Euthanasia 52

Chapter Nine: Abortion 61

Chapter Ten: The Death Penalty 64

Chapter Eleven: War or Peace 69

Section Four: The Importance of Holiness 73

Chapter Twelve: The Fruit of the Spirit 74

Chapter Thirteen: Clothing 78

Chapter Fourteen: Apparel 83

Chapter Fifteen: Coverings 95

Chapter Sixteen: The Results of Unholy Living 102

Section Five: Prophecy 105
Chapter Seventeen: The Rapture & Tribulation 106
Appendices 117
   Appendix One: The Nine Gifts of the Spirit 117
   Appendix Two: The Tribulation 121
References 124
Other Publications 126

Introduction

This is the fourth revised edition of this book. The content has not changed drastically; rather additional information within certain sections has been added to provide more clarity. I am not an author or a Biblical scholar, but by the grace of God, I have written this book to help people who question specific ethical and Biblical issues.

Despite one's age, race or even their intellectual ability we are all endowed with knowledge. Many of the topics in this book are straightforward but are essential for spiritual enlightenment. This book may offend some people, others may reject it, and some will accept it. Despite your reaction, we must know right from wrong. All the issues in this book are addressed from a Biblical perspective to increase your knowledge.

I have written this book to help Christians understand the Word of God. It is necessary to understand the Word of God and to apply it. Reading this book will help you come to the realization of the real heaven and hell issues and the correct standard of God.

Section One: The Importance of Spirituality

Abstract of section

Before analyzing the issues in this book, it is essential that we have a meaningful relationship with God. Once a relationship is established, we can proceed to deal with the spiritual, doctrinal and ethical issues presented in this book. This particular section focuses on building a spiritual foundation, understanding and applying the standard of God, and how we can contribute to the Kingdom of God.

Chapter One	A Spiritual Foundation
Chapter Two	Applying God's Standard
Chapter Three	Ministries

Chapter One: A Spiritual Foundation

The Bible mentions two men: one wise and one foolish. The wise one builds his house on the Rock, which is Christ Jesus and the foolish one builds on the earth. The house built on Jesus stood firm when a trial came while the home built on the earth crumbled when a test came because it was not built on the Rock *(Matthew 7:24-27[1])*.

During the duration of our lives, we acknowledge spiritual things because we all have spiritual awareness. Although we have spiritual awareness within, the most significant question is how do we build a spiritual foundation? Initially, we must believe that there is one true God and that there is only one way to be saved. Even though one of today's philosophies states that all roads lead to heaven, which is incorrect, salvation is via the gospel, which is by *(Acts 2:38[2])*:

1. Repentance from sins.
2. Baptism by immersion in the name of Jesus Christ *(Roman 6:4[3])*.
3. Receiving the gift of the Holy Ghost with the evidence of speaking in other tongues.

Understanding the Scriptures

Obeying this gospel fills the void within thus laying a true spiritual foundation which is built upon solid ground.

Some people argue about the deity of Jesus Christ, the gospel and other issues, but the Scriptures teach that there is no Trinity. Furthermore, everything should be done in the name of Jesus Christ.

Conclusively, acknowledging and obeying the gospel plants a person's feet on solid ground and if they continue on that path, Jesus will say "well-done" in eternity.

For further information on salvation and the oneness of God, please read *"The New Birth"* and *"The Oneness of God"* by David K. Bernard.

Allow me to expound on the statement, "there is no Trinity." Trinitarianism is the belief that there are three distinct persons in the Godhead. True apostolic believers do not believe in three separate beings being co-equal, co-eternal, or totally distinct persons who are separate from one another. Nor do we believe in binitarianism. Simply put, we believe in one true God. We believe that the Father, Son, and Holy Ghost are all one. God was manifest in the flesh, born

Chapter One: A Spiritual Foundation

of the Virgin Mary. In Jesus dwells all the fullness of the Godhead bodily. Jesus is the beginning of the creation of God, the firstborn of every creature; he is the incarnation of the unseen God, both in Heaven and on Earth *(Deuteronomy 6:4[4], Isaiah 43:10-11[5], Matthew 1:23[6], James 2:19[7], 1st Timothy 1:17[8], John 1:1, 10, 14[9], Colossians 1:15; 2:9[10], John 14:5-9[11], Isaiah 63:16[12], John 10:27-30[13], 1st John 5:7[14], 1st Timothy 3:16[15], Revelation 3:14[16]).*

---

[1] Therefore whosoever heareth these sayings of mine, and doeth them, I will liken him unto a wise man, which built his house upon a rock: 25: And the rain descended, and the floods came, and the winds blew, and beat upon that house; and it fell not: for it was founded upon a rock. 26: And every one that heareth these sayings of mine, and doeth them not, shall be likened unto a foolish man, which built his house upon the sand: 27: And the rain descended, and the floods came, and the winds blew, and beat upon that house; and it fell: and great was the fall of it (Matthew 7:24-27).

[2] Then Peter said unto them, Repent, and be baptized every one of you in the name of Jesus Christ for the remission of sins, and ye shall receive the gift of the Holy Ghost (Acts 2:38).

[3] Therefore we are buried with him by baptism into death: that like as Christ was raised up from the dead by the glory of the Father, even so we also should walk in newness of life (Romans 6:4).

[4] Hear, O Israel: The LORD our God is one LORD (Deuteronomy 6:4).

Understanding the Scriptures

―――――――――――――――――――――――――――――

⁵ Ye are my witnesses, saith the LORD, and my servant whom I have chosen: that ye may know and believe me, and understand that I am he: *before me there was no God formed, neither shall there be after me. 11: I, even I, am the LORD; and beside me there is no saviour (Isaiah 43:10-11).*

⁶ Behold, a virgin shall be with child, and shall bring forth a son, and they shall call his name Emmanuel, which being interpreted is, God with us (Matthew 1:23).

⁷ Thou believest that *there is one God;* thou doest well: the devils also believe, and tremble (James 2:19)

⁸ Now unto the King eternal, immortal, invisible, *the only wise God, be* honour and glory for ever and ever. Amen (1st Timothy 1:17).

⁹ In the beginning was the Word, and the Word was with God, and the Word was God. 10: He (Jesus) was in the world, and the world was made by him (Jesus), and the world knew him not. 14: And the Word (God) was made flesh, and dwelt among us, (and we beheld his glory, the glory as of the only begotten of the Father,) full of grace and truth (John 1:1, 10, 14).

¹⁰ Who is the image of the invisible God, the firstborn of every creature: 2:9: For in him (Jesus) dwelleth all the fulness of the Godhead bodily (Colossians 1:15; 2:9).

¹¹ Thomas saith unto him, Lord, we know not whither thou goest; and how can we know the way? 6: Jesus saith unto him, I am the way, the truth, and the life: no man cometh unto the Father, but by me. 7: If ye had known me, ye should have known my Father also: and from henceforth ye know him, and have seen him. 8: Philip saith unto him, Lord, shew us the Father, and it sufficeth us. 9: Jesus saith unto him, Have I been so long time with you, and yet hast thou not known me, Philip? *he that hath*

Chapter One: A Spiritual Foundation

seen me hath seen the Father; and how sayest thou *then,* Shew us the Father (John 14:5-9).

[12] Doubtless thou *art* our father, though Abraham be ignorant of us, and Israel acknowledge us not: thou, O LORD, *art* our father, our redeemer; thy name *is* from everlasting (Isaiah 63:16).

[13] My sheep hear my voice, and I know them, and they follow me: 28: And I give unto them eternal life; and they shall never perish, neither shall any *man* pluck them out of my hand. 29: My Father, which gave *them* me, is greater than all; and no *man* is able to pluck *them* out of my Father's hand. 30: *I and my Father are one* (John 10:27-30).

[14] For there are three that bear record in heaven, the Father, the Word (God which was manifested in the flesh, in other words Jesus), and the Holy Ghost: and *these three are one* (1 John 5:7).

[15] And without controversy great is the mystery of godliness: **God was manifest in the flesh**, justified in the Spirit, seen of angels, preached unto the Gentiles, believed on in the world, received up into glory (1 Timothy 3:16).

[16] And unto the angel of the church of the Laodiceans write; These things saith the Amen, the faithful and true witness, the beginning of the creation of God (Revelation 3:14).

Chapter Two: Applying God's Standard

Our obedience to *Act 2:38* lays a solid foundation as mentioned; however our compliance to the gospel is the beginning of our walk with God. Afterward, it is mandatory to follow the guidelines presented in the Bible. Unfortunately, numerous people (sinners and Christians) do not follow these guidelines, thus are on the road to hell without realizing it. In this chapter, various Scriptures will be analyzed, and if we are found guilty of anything mentioned, repentance is mandatory if we genuinely want to make heaven our home.

Firstly, as Christians because of our financial responsibilities, everyone ought to work with the exception of those who have medical and/or mental conditions or who study full time *(Genesis 3:19[1], Exodus 20:9; 23:12; 34:21[2], Leviticus 23:3[3], Deuteronomy 24:14[4], 2nd Chronicles 15:7[5], Proverbs 12:24; 13:4; 14:23; 21:25; 28:19[6], Ecclesiastes 5:12[7], 1st Timothy 5:18[8], Luke 10:7[9], Ephesians 4:28[10], and Colossians 3:22-23[11])*. As Christians, we are to spend money wisely, invest or save *(Matthew 25:24-26[12])*. In addition, we should not gamble and we should give ten percent of our

Chapter Two: Applying God's Standard

earnings to God *(Genesis 14:20; 28:20, 22[13], Leviticus 27:30, 32[14], Deuteronomy 12:6; 14:22, 28-29[15], 2nd Chronicles 31:5, 12[16], Amos 4:4[17], Malachi 3:8-10[18], and Hebrews 7:5[19]).* Some people state that it is not necessary to tithe because this was a part of the Levitical priesthood. Although this is true, tithing started before the law; thus we still ought to give our tithes. Jewish people have a motto which says, "ten percent to God and ten percent to me." This motto teaches us the principle of giving and saving. For further information on finances, please read, *"The Best Question Ever"* by Andy Stanley and, *"The Total Money Make Over"* by Dave Ramsey.

Secondly, Christians must live according to the various principles found in the Word. We should not defile our bodies or spirit because *1st Corinthians 6:9-10[20]* and *Galatians 5:19-21[21],* clearly state that people who commit the following sins will not enter the kingdom of God.

NOTE: Unless otherwise specified all definitions are taken from the Webster's Dictionary.

1. **Fornication:** *"Sexual intercourse between two people who are not married to each other."* According to the

New Testament Greek lexicon, the word fornication is, *"Porneia"* which refers to, premarital sex, bestiality, necrophilia (sex with the dead), homosexuality, masturbation, etc. Sexual relations other than what God has ordained and blessed are morally wrong. Also, note that enjoying sin is a type of fornication.

2. **Idolatry:** *"A worshipping of idols or intense admiration or love for something."* Anything you put before God is idol worship. It can be your car, house, television, etc.

3. **Adultery:** *"Voluntary sexual intercourse between a married person and someone other than his or her spouse."* Ruth 1:16-17 says, *"...Intreat me not to leave thee, or to return from following after thee: for whither thou goest, I will go; and where thou lodgest, I will lodge: thy people shall be my people, and thy God my God: 17: Where thou diest, will I die, and there will I be buried: the LORD do so to me, and more also, if ought but death part thee and me."* This portion of the Bible is a plea from Ruth to Naomi showing Ruth's commitment. Similarly, when we vow in marriage it is until death and breaking that covenant is contrary to the Bible.

Chapter Two: Applying God's Standard

4. **Effeminate:** *"Having or showing qualities that are considered more suitable to women than to men: not manly."* Please read my book *Overcoming Lust*, for detailed elaboration on the issue of transsexualism. People who cross-dress or are confused about their physical makeup cannot go to heaven unless they change. Nowadays men try to be effeminate, and women try to be masculine, but this is incorrect because it compromises God's standard. Repentance is mandatory for those who are effeminate. It is important to note that we do not disrespect people. We love the sinner and hate the sin.

5. **Abusers of themselves with mankind:** This comes from the Greek word, *"arsenokoites"* and it is defined in the New Testament Greek lexicon as, *"one who lies with a male as with a female, sodomite, homosexual."* Homosexuals and lesbians will not enter the kingdom of God. Note that this is the very reason why God destroyed Sodom and Gomorrah. Please refer to *Overcoming Lust* for details on this topic. Once again we love the sinner and hate the sin.

6. **Thieves:** *"One that steals."* All those who do not pay tithes, violate copyright laws, steal candy from a store, do

not pay taxes and so forth are considered thieves.

7. **Covetous:** *"Marked by a too eager desire especially for another's possessions."* As Christians, we should not envy what others have or desire to possess what they have.

8. **Drunkards**: *"A person who makes a habit of getting drunk."* Drunkards also include social and moderate drinking. Many believe it is acceptable to consume alcohol, but it is not acceptable. The Bible discourages the use of alcohol; however, some verses seem to encourage it. For instance, some state that Jesus turned water into wine *(John 2:1-10[22])*. The Bible says drunkards cannot enter heaven nor can they be filled with His spirit *(Ephesians 5:18[23])*. Furthermore, while on the cross Jesus was offered wine, but refused to drink it *(Matthew 27:34[24])*. Others reference *1st Timothy 5:23[25]* to justify their sinful actions. First of all, the word wine in the Bible has three meanings two of which are in Hebrew and one in Greek. In Hebrew *Tiyrâh* (unfermented) and *Yayin* (fermented or unfermented) whereas in Greek *Oinos* originates from the Hebrew word *Yayin*. Consequently, Jesus turned water into juice whereas Timothy was referring to wine for

Chapter Two: Applying God's Standard

medicinal purposes because he noted that leaders should not consume alcohol *(1st Timothy 3:1-12)*. In short, to understand this subject an analysis of each verse referring to wine in the Bible is necessary.

9. **Revilers**: *"To speak to or about in an insulting way."* When communicating with others, we ought to respect them even if they dislike or hate us. Furthermore, when talking with someone about another individual, we should reframe from saying negative things about anyone. If you have nothing good to say do not say anything at all.

10. **Extortionist:** *"The practice or crime of extorting (as money)."* As Christians, we need to be honest when it comes to money. The love of money is the root of all evil *(1st Timothy 6:10[26])*.

11. **Lasciviousness:** *"Excited by lust."* Lust is usually based on bad thoughts, traditionally based on sexual desires. If lust is not eliminated, it will destroy you. Please read my book titled: *Overcoming Lust*, for detailed elaboration on the issues of lust.

12. **Variance:** *"Not in harmony or agreement."* As children of God, we need to be in unity with everyone despite circumstances *(Psalms 133:1[27])*.

13. **Seditions:** *"The stirring up of feelings against lawful authority."* The law may seem corrupt, but obedience to the laws of the land is mandatory. We can voice our opinion, but it must be done respectfully. *Romans 13:1-7*[28] gives us instructions concerning the law.

14. **Heresies**: *"Religious opinion that is opposed to the doctrines of a church."* Exodus 23:7 says, *"Keep thee far from a false matter...for I will not justify the wicked."* There are many false doctrines, but there is only one church. Be wise and keep far from false doctrines because God will judge those who twist His Word and oppose the truth.

15. **Revellings:** *"To take part in a revel* (to party or get drunk), *be noisy in a festive* (joyful) *manner."* Going to secular parties and enjoying inappropriate music, alcohol or drugs is immoral. We need to ensure our spiritual safety by avoiding immorality. *"Thou shalt not follow a multitude to do evil..." (Exodus 13:2).*

16. **Witchcraft:** *"The use of sorcery or magic."* Christians need to avoid witchcraft including horoscopes and other sources of sorcery or magic such as eating fortune cookies and proceeding to read the fortune. If we do not go to

Chapter Two: Applying God's Standard

fortunetellers why would we read fortunes in a cookie?

17. **Emulations:** According to the Canadian Oxford Dictionary, *"desire to equal or excel others, imitate zealously and rival."* Emulating someone is appropriate when the person has good intentions. For instance, emulating your pastor is a good desire; nevertheless, when our motives are impure, we are sinning. When endeavoring to be like someone, it is necessary to remain humble and to have pure motives. Emulation also refers to having an enemy, which as established earlier is incorrect.

18. **Wrath:** *"Violent anger."* The Bible says, *"Be ye angry, and sin not..." (Ephesians 4:26).* If we do not control anger, it may lead to violence.

19. **Strife:** *"Bitter sometimes violent disagreement."* Bitter people cannot go to heaven. There should be no friction between Christians and others no matter what has happened. Strife within could lead to being violent.

20. **Hatred:** This is when you dislike someone, and the Bible refers to haters as murderers *(1st John 3:15[29]). Ephesians 4:31-32* says, *"Let all bitterness, and wrath, and anger, and clamour, and evil speaking, be put away from you, with all malice: And be ye kind one to another,*

tenderhearted, forgiving one another, even as God for Christ's sake hath forgiven you."

Conclusion

Luke 21:34[30] declares that the day of the Lord will come suddenly if we do not observe the commands of the Scripture. People who blasphemy, lie, are proud, have evil imaginations, cause discord, unbalanced, foolish, fearful, unbelieving, whoremongers and so forth will have their part in the lake of fire *(Colossians 3:8, 25[31], Proverbs 6:16-19; 11:1; 19:29; 24:9[32]* and *Revelation 21:8[33]).* If we sin we will miss the rapture or die in our iniquities, thus we need to repent and be vigilant to overcome the vices of the devil. Frequently we overlook these things thinking we are acceptable in God's sight. We need to search and examine ourselves daily *(Psalm 139:24[34])* to see if there is wickedness within because we cannot enter heaven if we live in sin. If we refuse to repent, we will be lost for eternity.

---

[1] In the sweat of thy face shalt thou eat bread… (Genesis 3:19).

[2] Six days shalt thou labour, and do all thy work…23:12: Six days thou shalt do thy work…34:21: Six days thou shalt work (Exodus 20:9; 23:12; 34:21).

Chapter Two: Applying God's Standard

³ Six days shall work be done…(Leviticus 23:3).

⁴ Thou shalt not oppress an hired servant (worker)…(Deuteronomy 24:14).

⁵ Be ye strong therefore, and let not your hands be weak: for your work shall be rewarded (2nd Chronicles 15:7).

⁶ Those who work hard…13:4: Those who work hard get plenty. If you work hard, you will have plenty…14:23: Whoever works hard will have plenty to eat….(Proverbs 12:24; 13:4; 14:23 ERV).

⁷ The sleep of a labouring man is sweet….(Ecclesiastes 5:12).

⁸ …The labourer is worthy of his reward (1st Timothy 5:18).

⁹ …for the labourer is worthy of his hire…(Luke 10:7).

¹⁰ Let him that stole steal no more: but rather let him labour, working with his hands the thing which is good, that he may have to give to him that needeth (Ephesians 4:28).

¹¹ Servants (workers), obey in all things your masters…23: And whatsoever ye do, do it …as to the Lord, and not unto men (Colossians 3:22-23).

¹² Then he which had received the one talent…25…was afraid, and went and hid thy talent in the earth…26: His lord answered and said unto him, Thou wicked and slothful servant…Thou oughtest therefore to have put my money to the exchangers…(Matthew 25:24-26).

¹³ …he (Abraham) gave him tithes of all. 28:20: And Jacob vowed a vow…22…I will

Understanding the Scriptures

surely give the tenth unto thee (Genesis 14:20; 28:20, 22).

[14] And all the tithe …32…the tenth shall be holy unto the LORD (Leviticus 27:30, 32).

[15] …your tithes, and…offerings…14:22: Thou shalt truly tithe…14:28…bring forth all the tithe of thine increase…14:29…that the LORD thy God may bless thee in all the work of thine hand which thou doest (Deuteronomy 12:6; 14:22, 28-29).

[16] …the tithe of all things brought they in abundantly…12: And brought in the offerings and the tithes… (2nd Chronicles 31:5, 12).

[17] … bring your…tithes… (Amos 4:4).

[18] Will a man rob God? Yet ye have robbed me…In tithes and offerings. 10: Bring ye all the tithes into the storehouse, that there may be meat in mine house, and prove me now herewith, saith the LORD of hosts, if I will not open you the windows of heaven, and pour you out a blessing, that there shall not be room enough to receive it (Malachi 3:8, 10).

[19] …take tithes of the people… (Hebrews 7:5).

[20] Know ye not that the unrighteous shall not inherit the kingdom of God? Be not deceived: neither fornicators, nor idolaters, nor adulterers, nor effeminate, nor abusers of themselves with mankind, Nor thieves, nor covetous, nor drunkards, nor revilers, nor extortioners, shall inherit the kingdom of God (1st Corinthians 6:9-10).

[21] Now the works of the flesh are manifest, which are these; Adultery, fornication, uncleanness, lasciviousness, 20: Idolatry, witchcraft, hatred, variance, emulations, wrath, strife, seditions, heresies, 21: Envyings, murders, drunkenness, revellings, and such like: of the which I tell you before, as I have also told you in time past, that they which do such things shall not inherit the kingdom of God (Galatians 5:19-21).

Chapter Two: Applying God's Standard

---

[22] And the third day there was a marriage in Cana of Galilee; and the mother of Jesus was there: 2: And both Jesus was called, and his disciples, to the marriage. 3: And when they wanted wine, the mother of Jesus saith unto him, They have no wine. 4: Jesus saith unto her, Woman, what have I to do with thee? mine hour is not yet come. 5: His mother saith unto the servants, Whatsoever he saith unto you, do it. 6: And there were set there six waterpots of stone, after the manner of the purifying of the Jews, containing two or three firkins apiece. 7: Jesus saith unto them, Fill the waterpots with water. And they filled them up to the brim. 8: And he saith unto them, Draw out now, and bear unto the governor of the feast. And they bare it. 9: When the ruler of the feast had tasted the water that was made wine, and knew not whence it was: (but the servants which drew the water knew;) the governor of the feast called the bridegroom, 10: And saith unto him, Every man at the beginning doth set forth good wine; and when men have well drunk, then that which is worse: but thou hast kept the good wine until now (John 2:1-10).

[23] And be not drunk with wine, wherein is excess; but be filled with the Spirit (Ephesians 5:18).

[24] They gave him vinegar to drink mingled with gall: and when he had tasted thereof, he would not drink (Matthew 27:34).

[25] Drink no longer water, but use a little wine for thy stomach's sake and thine often infirmities (1st Timothy 5:23).

[26] For the love of money is the root of all evil: which while some coveted after, they have erred from the faith, and pierced themselves through with many sorrows (1st Timothy 6:10).

Understanding the Scriptures

[27] Behold, how good and how pleasant it is for brethren to dwell together in unity (Psalms 133:1).

[28] Let every soul be subject unto the higher powers. For there is no power but of God: the powers that be are ordained of God. 2: Whosoever therefore resisteth the power, resisteth the ordinance of God: and they that resist shall receive to themselves damnation. 3: For rulers are not a terror to good works, but to the evil. Wilt thou then not be afraid of the power? do that which is good, and thou shalt have praise of the same: 4: For he is the minister of God to thee for good. But if thou do that which is evil, be afraid; for he beareth not the sword in vain: for he is the minister of God, a revenger to execute wrath upon him that doeth evil. 5: Wherefore ye must needs be subject, not only for wrath, but also for conscience sake. 6: For this cause pay ye tribute also: for they are God's ministers, attending continually upon this very thing. 7: Render therefore to all their dues: tribute to whom tribute is due; custom to whom custom; fear to whom fear; honour to whom honour (Romans 13:1-7).

[29] Whosoever hateth his brother is a murderer: and ye know that no murderer hath eternal life abiding in him (1st John 3:15).

[30] ...take heed...that day come upon you unawares (Luke 21:34).

[31] But now ye also put off all these; anger, wrath, malice, blasphemy, filthy communication out of your mouth. 25: But he that doeth wrong shall receive for the wrong which he hath done: and there is no respect of persons (Colossians 3:8, 25).

[32] These six things doth the LORD hate: yea, seven are an abomination unto him: 17: A proud look, a lying tongue, and hands that shed innocent blood, 18: An heart that deviseth wicked imaginations, feet that be swift in running to mischief, 19: A false witness that speaketh lies, and he that soweth discord among brethren. 11:1: A false

Chapter Two: Applying God's Standard

balance is abomination to the LORD: but a just weight is his delight 19:29: Judgments are prepared for scorners, and stripes for the back of fools. 24:9: The thought of foolishness is sin: and the scorner is an abomination to men (Proverbs 6:16-19; 11:1; 19:29; 24:9).

[33] But the fearful, and unbelieving, and the abominable, and murderers, and whoremongers, and sorcerers, and idolaters, and all liars, shall have their part in the lake which burneth with fire and brimstone: which is the second death (Revelation 21:8).

[34] And see if there be any wicked way in me, and lead me in the way everlasting (Psalms 139:24).

Chapter Three: Ministries

In the first chapter we looked at how to build a foundation, in the second chapter we analyzed various Scriptures, and now, we shall explore the different types of ministries that Christians can contribute to because working for His Kingdom is an obligation *(Mark 16:15[1])*. There are many ministries, and the goal of each department is to save souls and to encourage our fellow brothers and sisters.

The different types of ministries

1. In *Ephesians 4:11[2],* there is the fivefold ministry which is apostles, prophets, evangelists, pastors, and teachers.
    - An apostle is a church planter, a pioneer and a church builder who watches over the strict implementation of the doctrine of Jesus Christ and most of the time does missionary work. For instance, Paul was an apostle who went on missionary journeys planting churches.
    - Prophets carry the church or nation into the future by giving divine directions as revealed by the Lord.
    - Evangelists/missionaries spread the Word wherever they go for the sole purpose of winning the lost to

Christ.
- Pastors are the shepherds and leaders of the flock of God.
- Teachers build and grow the flock into maturity through profound revelations from teaching and expounding the Word of God.

2. *1st Timothy 3:1-12*[3] shows the office of bishops and deacons, and each of these offices and ministries is still operational today.
   - Bishops are overseers of a group of churches and pastors.
   - Deacons responsibilities vary and most often focus on the day to day activities of the church.

3. Women's ministry: men and women are permitted to preach and teach the gospel. Some state that women cannot preach or teach and use *1st Timothy 2:11-12*[4] and *1st Corinthians 14:34-35*[5] as references, however, these verses mean that women (wives) should not have an authoritative role over men (husbands). In regards to teaching and preaching, God used many women in the past. Some examples are Deborah in *Judges 4* and *5,* Queen Esther in the book of Esther, Miriam the

prophetess in *Exodus 15:20*[6] and women reported the resurrection of Jesus Christ (*Luke 24:9-10*[7]). Furthermore, *1st Corinthians 11* refers to women praying and prophesying in the church; consequently, women have the right to preach and teach the gospel.

4. In *1st Corinthians 12:28*[8], there is also the ministries of miracles, gifts of healings, helps, church government, and diversities of tongues all of which are used to edify the church or to bring the lost to salvation.

    - Church government is a group of board members who ensure that the affairs of the church are in order.
    - Helps ministry consist of people contributing their time, services and money to the advancement of the Kingdom.
    - The other ministries/gifts are explained in appendix one as well as the nine gifts of the Holy Spirit *(1st Corinthians 12:7-11)*.

5. Another department of ministry is counseling. Many individuals believe that counseling discredits the work of the Holy Spirit. Nonetheless, there are many Scriptural references for counseling. Some refer to professional

Chapter Three: Ministries

counseling and others refer to the counsel of the Holy Spirit *(Psalm 73:24[9], Proverbs 24:6[10], Isaiah 9:6[11], Romans 15:14[12], 2nd Corinthians 1:4[13], 1st Thessalonians 5:14[14], and Hebrews 3:13[15])*. In general there are two types of counseling: first, pastoral counseling, which focuses on applying Biblical truths. Second, secular counseling, which is the application of psychological methods. Christian counseling sometimes involves psychological methods viewed from a Christian perspective. Counseling must be based on Biblical principles, not secular ones. As Christians, we believe in the counsel of the Holy Spirit, but occasionally we need help from someone within the ministry who is mature and has vast experience. For instance, someone who is struggling to overcome sexual addictions may sincerely seek God but may need advice. This is not discrediting the work of the Spirit. Quite the opposite, the counselor helps this person by giving them sound advised based on Biblical principles as guided by the Holy Spirit. Overall, for counseling to be effective, it must be led by the Holy Spirit. The counseling ministry is very fruitful and helpful; however, there are a few ethics to remember:

Understanding the Scriptures

- Counselors are obligated to keep confidentiality. However, privacy can be broken if we are asked to lie, cheat or do something contrary to the Bible or if an individual wants to harm themselves or others.
- Counselors should not gossip or divulge secrets, *"A gossip betrays a confidence, but a trustworthy man keeps a secret" (Proverbs 11:13 NIV).*
- Counselors should not manipulate people for selfish gains such as extorting money in the name of special prayers.

In short, we all have a role to play within the body of Christ and our goal ought to be to win souls. If you lack or have no vision for soul winning, pray that God gives you one because *"Where there is no vision, the people perish..." (Proverbs 29:18).*

---

[1] And he said unto them, Go ye into all the world, and preach the gospel to every creature (Mark 16:15).

[2] And he gave some, apostles; and some, prophets; and some, evangelists; and some, pastors and teachers (Ephesians 4:11).

[3] This is a true saying, If a man desire the office of a bishop, he desireth a good work. 2: A bishop then must be blameless, the husband of one wife, vigilant, sober, of good

Chapter Three: Ministries

behaviour, given to hospitality, apt to teach; 3: Not given to wine, no striker, not greedy of filthy lucre; but patient, not a brawler, not covetous; 4: One that ruleth well his own house, having his children in subjection with all gravity; 5: (For if a man know not how to rule his own house, how shall he take care of the church of God?) 6: Not a novice, lest being lifted up with pride he fall into the condemnation of the devil. 7: Moreover he must have a good report of them which are without; lest he fall into reproach and the snare of the devil. 8: Likewise must the deacons be grave, not doubletongued, not given to much wine, not greedy of filthy lucre; 9: Holding the mystery of the faith in a pure conscience. 10: And let these also first be proved; then let them use the office of a deacon, being found blameless. 11: Even so must their wives be grave, not slanderers, sober, faithful in all things. 12: Let the deacons be the husbands of one wife, ruling their children and their own houses well (1st Timothy 3:1-12).

[4] Let the woman learn in silence with all subjection. 12: But I suffer not a woman to teach, nor to usurp authority over the man, but to be in silence (1st Timothy 2:11-12).

[5] Let your women keep silence in the churches: for it is not permitted unto them to speak; but they are commanded to be under obedience, as also saith the law. 35: And if they will learn any thing, let them ask their husbands at home: for it is a shame for women to speak in the church (1st Corinthians 14:34-35).

[6] …Miriam the prophetess… (Exodus 15:20).

[7] And returned from the sepulchre, and told all these things unto the eleven, and to all the rest. 10: It was Mary Magdalene, and Joanna, and Mary the mother of James, and other women that were with them, which told these things unto the apostles (Luke 24:9-10).

Understanding the Scriptures

⁸ But the manifestation of the Spirit is given to every man to profit withal. 8: For to one is given by the Spirit the word of wisdom; to another the word of knowledge by the same Spirit; 9: To another faith by the same Spirit; to another the gifts of healing by the same Spirit; 10: To another the working of miracles; to another prophecy; to another discerning of spirits; to another divers kinds of tongues; to another the interpretation of tongues: 11: But all these worketh that one and the selfsame Spirit, dividing to every man severally as he will…28: miracles, then gifts of healings, helps, governments, diversities of tongues (1st Corinthians 12:7-11, 28).

⁹ I will bless the LORD, who hath given me counsel…Thou shalt guide me with thy counsel…(Psalms 73:24).

¹⁰ …in multitude of counsellors there is safety (Proverbs 24:6).

¹¹ …his (Jesus) name shall be called…Counsellor…(Isaiah 9:6).

¹² …admonish one another (Romans 15:14). Sometimes this is done in counseling sessions.

¹³ …comfort (counsel/help) them which are in any trouble…(2nd Corinthians 1:4). Helping people is what counselors do.

¹⁴ …support the weak, be patient toward all men (1st Thessalonians 5:14). The weak are sometimes supported by seeing a counselor.

¹⁵ …exhort one another….(Hebrews 3:13). This is sometimes done in counseling relationships.

Section Two: Traditions

Abstract of section

Countless traditions can impact our spiritual foundation because every religion, culture, and individual has specific norms they follow. God also has specific criteria that Christians should follow. Nevertheless, often we do not comprehend the standard of God. For that reason, the focus of this section is to enlighten us on the norms of God with regards to the subjects below.

Chapter Four	Law or Grace
Chapter Five	Rituals
Chapter Six	Holidays

Chapter Four: Law or Grace

Many people are uncertain about the law of God and the grace of God, but this chapter will clarify this subject. The focus of this chapter is food, the law, the new covenant and the Sabbath day. The Bible says, *"God is not the author of confusion..." (1st Corinthians 14:33)*. Furthermore, *John 5:39*[1] encourages us to search the Scriptures to eliminate confusion and doubt. Studying the issues presented in this chapter is mandatory.

1. **Food**: We all eat, thus we agree that food is essential. Under the law (Old Testament), animals were killed to obtain a source of food, but certain foods were forbidden. Under grace (New Testament) some suggest that we can eat anything because we are no longer under the law. Unquestionably we are in the age of grace; however, does this mean we can eat anything? To answer that question lets analyze the Scriptures. In *Acts 10*, Peter had a vision and referred to the animals as unclean; however, Jesus said, *"rise, kill and eat."* Peter refused to do so because he kept the law. Jesus said the animals in the vision were not unclean or uncommon because they were blessed. First of all, this vision was to prepare Peter to eventually

Chapter Four: Law or Grace

witness to Cornelius because all prejudice had to be eliminated. Nevertheless, it does not eradicate the *"rise, kill and eat"* statement. Do these four words permit us to eat anything? In *Acts 15:5* the Pharisees believed that Gentiles needed to obey the law. *"But there rose up certain of the sect of the Pharisees which believed, saying...keep the law of Moses."* This complicated the issue therefore to solve this problem the apostles had a meeting. Following the meeting, it was concluded that we should adhere to the following.

- **Abstain from the pollution of idols:** This means believers should not eat meat that has been offered to idols. If we eat something that was offered to an idol unintentionally there will be no repercussions, nonetheless if we eat meat that was offered to an idol voluntarily and this offends others, we wound their weak consciences, thus for their sake we do not eat it *(1st Corinthians 8:1-13^2)*. According to Bernard (1985), *"Since an idol is nothing, there is nothing inherently immoral or dangerous about eating food that someone had offered to an idol. However, if others saw a Christian eating food offered to idols, they probably would interpret* *it as endorsing or condoning idol worship. For their sakes, therefore, Paul told the Corinthians not to eat food that they knew was offered to idols"* (p. 93).

- **Abstain from things strangled.**
- **Abstain from blood.**

To conclude, we can eat everything, but there are some basic guidelines. Consequently abstaining from certain foods and following strict principles is a personal choice. The Bible notes, *"...every creature of God is good, and nothing to be refused, if it be received with thanksgiving: 5: For it is sanctified by the word of God and prayer"* (1st Timothy 4:4-5). We need food to survive, and nowadays it is hard to find good quality food because most foods have either been genetically modified, has blood in it, has not been appropriately killed, etc. Going organic or becoming kosher is a personal choice. Often we are unaware of how food is prepared, and if you feel uncomfortable that certain foods do not meet the qualifications of the Scriptures, you need to pray and ask God to help you make the proper choices.

2. **The law and the new covenant**: Primarily the law was not destroyed, but fulfilled when Christ came. *"Think not that I am come to destroy the law, or the prophets: I am*

Chapter Four: Law or Grace

not come to destroy, but to fulfil" (Matthew 5:17). Galatians 3:24 refers to the law as our schoolmaster, but this schoolmaster brought us to Christ and through faith we are made right with God. Christ brought us into the age of grace setting us free from the bondage of sin and death, but did grace destroy the law? The law was not destroyed, but fulfilled and as Christians, we are to follow in the footsteps of Jesus by obeying the laws of God. For instance, we obey the Ten Commandments because these laws are still in place despite the coming of Christ. Why do we obey these laws? According to Reynolds (1987), Christians obey the Ten Commandments because Christ dwells within our hearts. He goes onto to state that Christians do not live righteously to become righteous, rather Christians live righteously because they are already made righteous. While studying this subject, it is essential to understand what laws are applicable and inapplicable. There are three types of laws:

- First, the social laws that governed Israel for a particular period, therefore these laws are irrelevant.
- Second, ceremonial laws that revealed God's salvation; these are also irrelevant because salvation is via the gospel

of Jesus Christ.

- Third, the moral laws which are enforced always and everywhere. According to Bernard (1985), *"Finally, we are specifically freed from the ceremonial law of the Old Testament (Mark 7:15[3]; Galatians 3:24-25; 4:9-11, 21-31[4]). God used the ceremonial law—including blood sacrifices, dietary laws, circumcision, sabbaths, and feasts—as types and foreshadowings of the truth to be found in Christ and His gospel"* (p. 90).

3. **The Sabbath day**: Traditions are created, or God made. God established the Sabbath day (Saturday) as the day of rest. Though we are freed from the traditions of the Sabbath, a day of rest is necessary, and I believe that we must take advantage of a good days rest when we have the chance. Nonetheless, it is vital that we do not get caught in the trap of the traditions of the Sabbath.

In conclusion, to be blessed we need to do what God asks. Following specific norms that are not found within the Bible is a personal choice, however, if it is mentioned in the Bible and we do not adhere to it, our foundation will become weak or may cause someone else to become weak, thus

Chapter Four: Law or Grace

endangering our eternal souls. Finally, if you are not sure about specific issues presented in this chapter, pray, seek God, study and He will reveal the truth unto you.

---

[1] Search the scriptures; for in them ye think ye have eternal life: and they are they which testify of me (John 5:39).

[2] Now as touching things offered unto idols, we know that we all have knowledge. Knowledge puffeth up, but charity edifieth. 2: And if any man think that he knoweth any thing, he knoweth nothing yet as he ought to know. 3: But if any man love God, the same is known of him. 4: As concerning therefore the eating of those things that are offered in sacrifice unto idols, we know that an idol is nothing in the world, and that there is none other God but one. 5: For though there be that are called gods, whether in heaven or in earth, (as there be gods many, and lords many,) 6: But to us there is but one God, the Father, of whom are all things, and we in him; and one Lord Jesus Christ, by whom are all things, and we by him. 7: Howbeit there is not in every man that knowledge: for some with conscience of the idol unto this hour eat it as a thing offered unto an idol; and their conscience being weak is defiled. 8: But meat commendeth us not to God: for neither, if we eat, are we the better; neither, if we eat not, are we the worse. 9: But take heed lest by any means this liberty of yours become a stumblingblock to them that are weak. 10: For if any man see thee which hast knowledge sit at meat in the idol's temple, shall not the conscience of him which is weak be emboldened to eat those things which are offered to idols; 11: And through thy knowledge shall the weak brother perish, for whom Christ died? 12: But when ye sin so against the brethren, and wound their weak conscience, ye sin against Christ. 13: Wherefore, if meat make my brother to offend, I will eat no flesh while the world standeth, lest I make my brother to offend (1st Corinthians 8:1-13).

³ There is nothing from without a man, that entering into him can defile him: but the things which come out of him, those are they that defile the man (Mark 7:15).

⁴ Wherefore the law was our schoolmaster to bring us unto Christ, that we might be justified by faith. 25: But after that faith is come, we are no longer under a schoolmaster. 4:9: But now, after that ye have known God, or rather are known of God, how turn ye again to the weak and beggarly elements, whereunto ye desire again to be in bondage? 10: Ye observe days, and months, and times, and years. 11: I am afraid of you, lest I have bestowed upon you labour in vain (Galatians 3:24-25; 4:9-11).

Chapter Five: Rituals

Overlooking rituals and traditions, and assuming they will not affect our foundation will be detrimental. Since having a good foundation is very important, we will now analyze two rituals: communion and the feet washing service. As Christians, we need to know why these two rituals are essential.

1. **Communion**: Communion is when we remember the sufferings of Christ. This was a system set up by Christ *(Matthew 26:26-28[1])*. Communion has a simple format. The bread represents the broken body of Christ, and we are to eat the bread. The juice represents the blood of Christ that was shed for us, and we are to drink the juice. In *1st Corinthians 11:23-30[2],* Paul talks about the requirements for communion. He noted that unworthy people (sinners or those living in sin) who take communion would face consequences, one of them being death, which would affect a person's foundation, which had already been weakened by sin. Communion is a time to remember what Christ did for us on the cross. This ritual is not to be taken lightly, and we must take it in

honesty and avoid it if necessary.

2. **Feet washing service**: The feet washing service, was also established by Christ *(John 13:1-15[3])*. The feet washing service is when we humble ourselves towards each other by washing each other's feet and this ought to be done after communion. This act allows us to practice being humble.

Conclusively, it is imperative for us to have an understanding of these rituals so as to be blessed. Often, we are unaware of what we are doing and why we are doing it.

---

[1] And as they were eating, Jesus took bread, and blessed it, and brake it, and gave it to the disciples, and said, Take, eat; this is my body. 27: And he took the cup, and gave thanks, and gave it to them, saying, Drink ye all of it; 28: For this is my blood of the new testament, which is shed for many for the remission of sins (Matthew 26:26-28).

[2] For I have received of the Lord that which also I delivered unto you, That the Lord Jesus the same night in which he was betrayed took bread: 24: And when he had given thanks, he brake it, and said, Take, eat: this is my body, which is broken for you: this do in remembrance of me. 25: After the same manner also he took the cup, when he had supped, saying, This cup is the new testament in my blood: this do ye, as oft as ye drink it, in remembrance of me. 26: For as often as ye eat this bread, and drink this cup, ye do shew the Lord's death till he come. 27: Wherefore whosoever shall eat this bread, and drink this cup of the Lord, unworthily, shall be guilty of the body and blood of the Lord. 28: But let a man examine himself, and so let him eat of

Chapter Five: Rituals

that bread, and drink of that cup. 29: For he that eateth and drinketh unworthily, eateth and drinketh damnation to himself, not discerning the Lord's body. 30: For this cause many are weak and sickly among you, and many sleep (1st Corinthians 11:23-30).

[3] Now before the feast of the passover, when Jesus knew that his hour was come that he should depart out of this world unto the Father, having loved his own which were in the world, he loved them unto the end. 2: And supper being ended, the devil having now put into the heart of Judas Iscariot, Simon's son, to betray him; 3: Jesus knowing that the Father had given all things into his hands, and that he was come from God, and went to God; 4: He riseth from supper, and laid aside his garments; and took a towel, and girded himself. 5: After that he poureth water into a bason, and began to wash the disciples' feet, and to wipe them with the towel wherewith he was girded. 6: Then cometh he to Simon Peter: and Peter saith unto him, Lord, dost thou wash my feet? 8: Jesus answered and said unto him, What I do thou knowest not now; but thou shalt know hereafter. Peter saith unto him, Thou shalt never wash my feet. Jesus answered him, If I wash thee not, thou hast no part with me. 9: Simon Peter saith unto him, Lord, not my feet only, but also my hands and my head. 10: Jesus saith to him, He that is washed needeth not save to wash his feet, but is clean every whit: and ye are clean, but not all. 11: For he knew who should betray him; therefore said he, Ye are not all clean. 12: So after he had washed their feet, and had taken his garments, and was set down again, he said unto them, Know ye what I have done to you? 13: Ye call me Master and Lord: and ye say well; for so I am. 14: If I then, your Lord and Master, have washed your feet; ye also ought to wash one another's feet. 15: For I have given you an example, that ye should do as I have done to you (John 13:1-15).

Chapter Six: Holidays

There are numerous religious and secular holidays celebrated, thus writing about all of them would be time-consuming. It is important to realize that whatever we do in the natural realm will affect us in the spiritual realm. If we are negatively affected in the spiritual realm, our foundation will eventually crumble. Consequently, it is essential to determine if we can or cannot celebrate certain holidays.

1. **Mothers and Fathers day:** These holidays can be celebrated because the Bible says in *Ephesians 6:1-2[1]* that children should honor their parents.
2. **Labor Day:** Labor Day is a day of rest; hence this day can be observed.
3. **Thanksgiving:** Thanksgiving is a time to give thanks, and the Bible encourages us to give thanks; hence people can observe this day *(1st Thessalonians 5:18[2])*.
4. **Palm and Easter Sunday:** Palm and Easter Sunday are two major holidays that Christians celebrate. Primarily, Christians should not believe in the Easter bunny or anything that originates from paganism. We celebrate these holidays to remember what Christ did for us on

Calvary and how powerful He is *(1st Corinthians 15:1-4 and Luke 19:35-38³)*.

5. **Remembrance Day:** Remembrance Day known as Veterans Day in America is when we honor those who died in a war. We do not agree with war, but at the same time, we give honor to those who fought and won the victory for the liberty we have *(Romans 13:7)*.

6. **New Year's Eve:** For the most part people celebrate this holiday while drinking or using drugs. Christians should not encourage or engage in such behaviors, but thanking God and being in church to celebrate this holiday is correct.

7. **Saint Patrick's Day:** This holiday involves people celebrating while drinking or using drugs. Saint Patrick preached about God and used a three-leafed shamrock to proclaim the concept of the Trinity. Nowadays, people worship Saint Patrick and the shamrock. As established in chapter two, it is incorrect to worship anything else other than God. Christians should not celebrate this holiday because worship is directed towards a person and not God. Moreover, the shamrock represents the Trinity which contradicts oneness belief; thus we cannot support

or celebrate this day.

8. **Birthdays:** In the Bible, Pharaoh and Herod celebrated their birthdays. On Pharaoh's birthday, he had his chief baker killed while Herod executed John the Baptist on his birthday *(Genesis 40:20-22[4] and Mark 6:17-28[5])*. Greeks and Romans celebrated the birthdays of gods, and as men became more powerful, they celebrated their birthdays. Pharaoh and Herod did evil on their birthdays, and the Greeks and Romans honored idols on their birthdays. Does all of this mean we should not celebrate our birthdays? In the Bible, there is nothing that indicates that we cannot celebrate birthdays. When we make it through another year, we celebrate because having life is the favor of God *(see Job 10:12)*. Celebrating while enjoying worldly pleasures is wrong; however, focusing on God and giving thanks is correct.

9. **Valentine's Day:** On this day people express their love; however, many sexual sins are committed on this day, and Cupid is the god of this holiday. God is the one who teaches us how to love not Cupid. Some people exchange genuine expressions of love on February 14th, which is acceptable if they are married. Nevertheless, should

Chapter Six: Holidays

Christians celebrate this day? According to Pack (2008), Valentine's Day was a pagan holiday known as *Lupercalia* (the festival of sexual license) and the feast day of *Juno,* the goddess. The festival was linked with the pagan practice of teenagers engaging in erotic encounters. In short, Christians should not encourage or approve of the evil customs of this day. However if a married couple desires to express their love towards each other on this day, that is acceptable. As long as we do not endorse or encourage sin or pagan customs, showing your love on this day is acceptable.

10. **Halloween:** As Christians, we should not celebrate Halloween because it glorifies everything that is evil because it involves fortunetelling, haunted houses, scary stories, and other evil customs. According to Pack (2002), two thousand years ago ancient Celts celebrated *Samhain* from October 31st to November 2nd. During this festival, they would sacrifice animals, vegetables, fruits, and light bonfires to honor the dead. Also, people wore costumes of animal skins and heads and attempted to tell each other's fortunes. Shall I go on? This holiday has nothing to do with God.

11. **Christmas:** Christmas is another controversial holiday, and many Christians are uncertain if they should celebrate this day or not. According to Pack (2008), he notes that ancient Romans celebrated a holiday called *Saturnalia*, which was from December 17-24 in honor of their god *Saturn*: the fire god. On December 25th pagans celebrated the birth of the unconquered sun as decreed by the emperor Aurelian in A.D. 274. During this holiday people decorated their homes, exchanged gifts, etc. First of all, it is important to note that Christ was not born on December 25th. Furthermore, Christmas trees, lights, gift exchanges, Santa Claus (Satan Claus) and so forth represent pagan customs. Some people try to justify tradition, but even the Bible discourages pagan customs: *"Do not act like the other nations...Their ways are futile and foolish. They cut down a tree...decorate it with gold and silver and then fasten it securely...so it won't fall over. 5. Their gods are like helpless scarecrows in a cucumber field! They cannot speak, and they need to be carried because they cannot walk..." (Jeremiah 10:2-5 NLT)*. It is interesting to note that the tree in *Jeremiah* is referred to as a god. When we put up a Christmas tree and lay gifts under it, it represents

Chapter Six: Holidays

idol worship. In short, if you celebrate or not that is a personal choice. I do not agree with the pagan customs as mentioned earlier, however, at Christmas many acknowledge Christ, and as believers, we can use that opportunity to help people come to the full knowledge of Jesus Christ. Furthermore, family dinners or fellowships can be used as a means to help people come to a understanding of Jesus Christ.

In short, some holidays can be celebrated while others cannot. All celebrations must be based on Scriptural principles so that we can avoid damaging our foundation.

---

[1] Children, obey your parents in the Lord: for this is right. 2: Honour thy father and mother; (which is the first commandment with promise) (Ephesians 6:1-2).

[2] In every thing give thanks: for this is the will of God in Christ Jesus concerning you (1st Thessalonians 5:18).

[3] And they brought him to Jesus: and they cast their garments upon the colt, and they set Jesus thereon. 36: And as he went, they spread their clothes in the way. 37: And when he was come nigh, even now at the descent of the mount of Olives, the whole multitude of the disciples began to rejoice and praise God with a loud voice for all the mighty works that they had seen; 38: Saying, Blessed be the King that cometh in the name of the Lord: peace in heaven, and glory in the highest (Luke 19:35-38).

Understanding the Scriptures

⁴ And it came to pass the third day, which was Pharaoh's birthday, that he made a feast unto all his servants: and he lifted up the head of the chief butler and of the chief baker among his servants. 21: And he restored the chief butler unto his butlership again; and he gave the cup into Pharaoh's hand: 22: But he hanged the chief baker: as Joseph had interpreted to them (Genesis 40:20-22).

⁵ For Herod himself had sent forth and laid hold upon John, and bound him in prison for Herodias' sake, his brother Philip's wife: for he had married her. 18: For John had said unto Herod, It is not lawful for thee to have thy brother's wife. 19: Therefore Herodias had a quarrel against him, and would have killed him; but she could not: 20: For Herod feared John, knowing that he was a just man and an holy, and observed him; and when he heard him, he did many things, and heard him gladly. 21: And when a convenient day was come, that Herod on his birthday made a supper to his lords, high captains, and chief estates of Galilee; 22: And when the daughter of the said Herodias came in, and danced, and pleased Herod and them that sat with him, the king said unto the damsel, Ask of me whatsoever thou wilt, and I will give it thee. 23: And he sware unto her, Whatsoever thou shalt ask of me, I will give it thee, unto the half of my kingdom. 24: And she went forth, and said unto her mother, What shall I ask? And she said, The head of John the Baptist. 25: And she came in straightway with haste unto the king, and asked, saying, I will that thou give me by and by in a charger the head of John the Baptist. 26: And the king was exceeding sorry; yet for his oath's sake, and for their sakes which sat with him, he would not reject her. 27: And immediately the king sent an executioner, and commanded his head to be brought: and he went and beheaded him in the prison, 28: And brought his head in a charger, and gave it to the damsel: and the damsel gave it to her mother (Mark 6:17-28).

Section Three: The Importance of Life

Abstract of section

Our focus thus far has been directed on keeping our spiritual foundation intact. In this section, we shall analyze ethical issues in relation to the Bible to bring out clear boundaries. When confronted by these issues unclear boundaries will produce doubt leading to double mindedness (sin), which will affect our spiritual foundation.

Chapter Seven	Against Nature
Chapter Eight	Euthanasia
Chapter Nine	Abortion
Chapter Ten	The Death Penalty
Chapter Eleven	War or Peace

Chapter Seven: Against Nature

When I began writing this section, I was unsure of what title to give this chapter. This chapter is titled against nature because the issues presented are against the nature of God. It is essential to understand that life is given by God, even if some erroneous theories try to dispute this fact.

The book of *Genesis* reveals how God created the world and how He established multiplication and fruitfulness *(Genesis 1:26-28)*. However, due to disobedience and sin, we face many consequences today. In a bit to solve this, man has established many scientific experiments which unfortunately opposes the very nature of creation. As Christians, it is essential to determine right from wrong. So we shall analyze some of these experiments to see how wrong they are:

1. **Cloning:** Cloning involves replicating an embryo to produce two identical individuals or animals. God is the one who gives life, and this starts at conception, and this system is the only acceptable method of reproduction. According to Got Questions Ministries, *"Many people believe that life does not begin at conception with the*

Chapter Seven: Against Nature

formation of the embryo, and therefore embryos are not really human beings. The Bible teaches differently according to Psalm 139:13-16." Life is valuable, and anything that compromises it must not be endorsed.

2. **Reproductive technology:** Reproductive technology also known as In Vitro Fertilization involves the mixing of the husband's sperm with the wife's egg in a test tube. If successful, embryos are produced, and one of them will be inserted into the woman's womb, which will hopefully develop into a baby. During this process, there are many embryos, but not all of them are used. The remaining ones are used for research purposes or are allowed to die which is incorrect. If the woman only received sperm from her husband without any embryos being killed, this process would be appropriate. Alternatively, some women receive sperm from another donor. This is incorrect because it is no different from a woman who commits adultery. As Christians, we need to be very careful with this type of technology.

3. **Transsexualism:** Transsexualism finds its roots connected to lust. This involves cross-dressing, sex changes, etc. Perhaps those with such behaviors have

psychological disorders? Only a psychologist can determine that. Or maybe they were born that way? This is not possible because in everyone's DNA and chromosomes they are either male or female. People with male and female physical characteristics usually undergo surgery or medications changed their natural makeup. This issue has brought about a lot of confusion, and it opposes God's creation. Scientist abuse their God-given talents and as Christians, we ought to oppose transsexualism because it is contrary to the Word of God *(1st Corinthians 6:9-10)*.

4. **Transgenics:** Transgenics is when the genetic makeup of animals is changed to make their organs compatible for human transplants. When God created Adam and Eve, they were sinless, healthy and immortal. Due to their disobedience sin was brought into the world, which leads to sickness and eventually death. Most people fear death and scientist are going to extremes to extend life. Medical treatment is correct such as antibiotics, but transgenics is inappropriate.

5. **Genetic engineering:** Genetic engineering is the manipulation of plants or animals to make them resistant

Chapter Seven: Against Nature

to disease, to be more productive or to become larger. First of all, such methods interfere with the natural processes of life. Second of all, is it possible that these experiments are causing all of or some the health problems people face such as cancers and Alzheimer's? The right way is the natural process, which was established by God.

To conclude, God created life and a perfect system, but sin destroyed what God made. The issues mentioned in this chapter are not Biblical neither is it the will of God that such customs are practiced. If we agree with any of the topics mentioned in this chapter, then the foundation we are trying to establish will become faulty because we have compromised the true standard of God.

Chapter Eight: Euthanasia

The previous chapter establishes that God gives life; however, do we have the power or the ability to terminate life? Undoubtedly everyone will face death *(Hebrews 9:27[1])*. Euthanasia, a controversial issue, enables people to determine when they will die, but the Bible says no one should kill *(Exodus 20:13[2])*. This issue has caused great debates, but it is essential to view it from God's perspective. We shall analyze it as follows:

1. **A detailed description of Euthanasia:** The first question that comes to mind is, "what is euthanasia and why the debate?" Euthanasia is voluntary (agreed to) or involuntary (not agreed to) termination of an individual's life. Webster's defines euthanasia as, *"the act or practice of killing or permitting the death of hopelessly sick or injured individuals (as persons or domestic animals) in a relatively painless way for reasons of mercy."* There is a debate because euthanasia is illegal in some parts of the world, it is not defined clearly, and the code of ethics refers to nonmaleficence[1] and autonomy[2]. Gentles (1995)

Chapter Eight: Euthanasia

in his book notes, *"Legalizing assisted suicide and euthanasia would be profoundly dangerous for many individuals who are ill and vulnerable" (p. 17)*. In 400 BC the father of medicine declared he would not give deadly medicine to anyone. Whether or not there is ever any clarification regarding this topic, it is important to identify what euthanasia is and is not. First, euthanasia is the process of painlessly helping a terminally ill person to die (this definition does not mention those who are mentally ill or unable to voice their opinion or if it is voluntary or involuntary). Generally, euthanasia is performed by lethal injection using the same drugs like those used to execute those on death row. Second, euthanasia is not refusing medical intervention or pulling the plug.

2. **The Historical context of Euthanasia:** The information above gives a general idea as to why there are debates.

---

[1] Nonmaleficence is not willfully harming people and/or abstaining from actions that risk harm.

[2] Autonomy is the freedom of choice.

Now let's examine the history of euthanasia. Euthanasia is referred to as assisted suicide or mercy killings. Minois (1995) states that in Plato's time suicide was forbidden unless it was mandatory, *"Plato forbade killing oneself, unless the gods made it necessary...As long as the body and mind enjoyed possessions of their full faculties and can live a worthy life, there is no reason to kill oneself...when afflicted with the decrepitude and sufferings of advanced old age...we have it in our power to deliver oneself from them"* (p. 48, 51-52). Assisted suicide has always been a subject of debate. The first recorded law regarding the band of euthanasia was established in 1828 in New York. In 1920, doctors Alfred Hoche and Karl Binding published a book titled, *"Permitting the Destruction of Life not Worthy of Life."* They believed in euthanasia under controlled conditions. Euthanasia began in 1935 in Britain, 1938 in America and 1939 during Hitler's reign euthanasia was used. According to Peck (1997), *"...The Nazi government in Germany put to death by gas or lethal injection 70,000 assorted people who were mentally retarded, schizophrenic, or senile. They referred to this...as the euthanasia program...the*

Chapter Eight: Euthanasia

Nazi's called it mercy killings" (p. 100). According to Peck (1997), the Nazi regime referred to the euthanasia program as merciful because the people being killed had a poor quality of life. In 1980, euthanasia began in Canada. In 1995, Australia's Northern Territory approved a euthanasia bill that went into effect in 1996 but was overturned by the Australian Parliament in 1997. In 1998, the U.S. state of Oregon legalized assisted suicide. In 1999, Dr. Jack Kevorkian was sentenced to prison for giving a lethal injection to Thomas Youk. In 2000, The Netherlands legalized euthanasia. In 2002, Belgium legalized it and in 2008, the U.S. state of Washington legalized assisted suicide. And, the saga continues today.

3. **The Bible and Euthanasia:** *Ecclesiastes 3:1[3]* says that there is a time and a purpose for everything. *Hebrews 9:27* says we all have an appointment with death. The Bible also notes *"no man has power over the…day of his death…" (Ecclesiastes 8:8 NIV).* God determines when life ends not us. *Ecclesiastes 7:17* states, *"… neither be thou foolish: why shouldest thou die before thy time?"* Dying before the appointed time is not sensible. There was a man in the Bible named Abner; he was murdered

and was considered foolish because of the choices he made *(2nd Samuel 3:27, 33[4])*. Abner died before his appointed time because he was not thinking logically. Those who receive or want to receive euthanasia treatment are not thinking logically. People state that it is cruel to let people suffer, however *Proverbs 31:6* states, *"Give strong drink unto him that is ready to perish, and wine unto those that be of heavy hearts."* Today we have many medications that can help relieve pain as strong drink did in Solomon's day. Certain medications or medical treatment can help those who are terminally ill. Although a person has the right to refuse medical treatment, they also have the right to accept it. God gives life while the devil destroys lives *(John 10:10[5])*. The devil possesses people who harm themselves. For instance, the man with a legion of devils hurt himself because he was possessed, but when he met Jesus his life changed *(Mark 5:1-15[6])*. Another example is Saul who while in battle begged his fellow soldier (his servant) to kill him, but the servant refused to do so, and as a result, Saul committed suicide *(1st Samuel 31:1-6[7])*. Afterward, an Amalekite claimed he killed Saul and was judged by God for his so-

Chapter Eight: Euthanasia

called actions *(2nd Samuel 1:1-16[8])*. Saul was in pain and wanted to die, but was he thinking logically? No, and his fellow soldier realized this, thus refusing to kill Saul. After Saul killed himself, the Amalekite who claimed to kill him was judged. If God judged the Amalekite who was innocent would He not also judge those who kill others? Others ask about the quality of life and the elderly. The Bible also gives instructions in these areas.

- Primarily, as people age the Scriptures instruct us to care for them *(Leviticus 19:32[9], Matthew 15:3-4[10], Ephesians 6:2, James 1:27[11] and 1st Timothy 5:4, 8[12])*.
- Secondly, the quality of life is not determined by how healthy or how sick a person is. Pain and suffering are not pleasant, but God's grace is sufficient in our weaknesses *(2nd Corinthians 12:9[13])*. Furthermore, suffering is not eradicated by death. If a suffering person dies and goes to hell the pain experienced while on earth will be the only heaven they would have ever known. Suffering eternally is a horrible thought. We focus on the temporal, and most of the time we do not think of eternity. Job suffered physically, but he refused to curse God and die, and life went on *(Job 2:9-10[14])*.

Understanding the Scriptures

In short, we must realize the importance of human life. Indeed life is temporary but remember that once we die eternity awaits us. If we endorse or agree with euthanasia, our foundation will be unstable, and as a result, we will face eternal consequences. The Bible declares in *John 16:33*[15] that in this life we will have tribulation and that includes sickness. Christians must oppose euthanasia because we believe in the preservation of life.

---

[1] And as it is appointed unto men once to die, but after this the judgment (Hebrews 9:27).

[2] Thou shalt not kill (Exodus 20:13).

[3] To every thing there is a season, and a time to every purpose under the heaven (Ecclesiastes 3:1).

[4] And when Abner was returned to Hebron, Joab took him aside in the gate to speak with him quietly, and smote him there under the fifth rib, that he died... 33: And the king lamented over Abner, and said, Died Abner as a fool dieth (2nd Samuel 3:27, 33).

[5] The thief cometh not, but for to steal, and to kill, and to destroy: I am come that they might have life, and that they might have it more abundantly (John 10:10).

[6] And they came over unto the other side of the sea, into the country of the Gadarenes.

Chapter Eight: Euthanasia

2: And when he was come out of the ship, immediately there met him out of the tombs a man with an unclean spirit, 3: Who had his dwelling among the tombs; and no man could bind him, no, not with chains: 4: Because that he had been often bound with fetters and chains, and the chains had been plucked asunder by him, and the fetters broken in pieces: neither could any man tame him. 5: And always, night and day, he was in the mountains, and in the tombs, crying, and cutting himself with stones. 6: But when he saw Jesus afar off, he ran and worshipped him, 9: And he (Jesus) asked him, What is thy name? And he answered, saying, My name is Legion: for we are many. 13: And forthwith Jesus gave them leave (rebuked the devils)...15: And they come to Jesus, and see him that was possessed with the devil, and had the legion, sitting, and clothed, and in his right mind... (Mark 5:1-6, 9, 13, 15).

[7] Now the Philistines fought against Israel: and the men of Israel fled from before the Philistines, and fell down slain in mount Gilboa. 2: And the Philistines followed hard upon Saul and upon his sons; and the Philistines slew Jonathan, and Abinadab, and Malchishua, Saul's sons. 3: And the battle went sore against Saul, and the archers hit him; and he was sore wounded of the archers. 4: Then said Saul unto his armourbearer, Draw thy sword, and thrust me through therewith; lest these uncircumcised come and thrust me through, and abuse me. But his armourbearer would not; for he was sore afraid. Therefore Saul took a sword, and fell upon it. 5: And when his armourbearer saw that Saul was dead, he fell likewise upon his sword, and died with him. 6: So Saul died, and his three sons, and his armourbearer, and all his men, that same day together (1st Samuel 31:1-6).

[8] Now it came to pass after the death of Saul...behold, a man came out of the camp from Saul...3...And David said unto him...5: ...How knowest thou that Saul and Jonathan his son be dead? 10... I stood upon him, and slew him...13: And David said unto the young man...14...How wast thou not afraid to stretch forth thine hand to destroy the LORD'S anointed? 15: And David called one of the young men, and said,

Understanding the Scriptures

Go near, and fall upon him. And he smote him that he died. 16: And David said unto him, Thy blood be upon thy head; for thy mouth hath testified against thee, saying, I have slain the LORD'S anointed (2nd Samuel 1:1, 3, 5, 10, 13, 14-16).

9 …honour the face of the old man, and fear thy God: I am the LORD (Leviticus 19:32).

10 But he answered and said unto them, Why do ye also transgress the commandment of God by your tradition? 4: For God commanded, saying, Honour thy father and mother: and, He that curseth father or mother, let him die the death (Matthew 15:3-4).

11 …visit the fatherless and widows in their affliction…(James 1:27).

12 But if any widow have children or nephews, let them learn first to shew piety at home, and to requite their parents: for that is good and acceptable before God. 8: But if any provide not for his own, and specially for those of his own house, he hath denied the faith, and is worse than an infidel (1st Timothy 5:4, 8).

13 And he said unto me, My grace is sufficient for thee: for my strength is made perfect in weakness. Most gladly therefore will I rather glory in my infirmities, that the power of Christ may rest upon me (2nd Corinthians 12:9).

14 Then said his wife unto him…curse God, and die. 10: But he said unto her, Thou speakest as one of the foolish women speaketh. What? shall we receive good at the hand of God, and shall we not receive evil? In all this did not Job sin with his lips (Job 2:9-10).

15 …In the world ye shall have tribulation: but be of good cheer; I have overcome the world (John 16:33).

Chapter Nine: Abortion

Euthanasia, as mentioned, is wrong because lives are terminated before the appointed time. Abortion also ends lives, but like euthanasia, the subject is debated by many. We shall therefore also analyze abortion from a Biblical perspective.

The medical dictionary defines abortion as, *"the premature exit of the products of conception (the fetus, fetal membranes, and placenta) from the uterus."* There are many ways that pregnancy is terminated and many women have had abortions. Some women abort because of pressure while others do so willingly.

Primarily, it is important to note that God will judge those who commit abortions voluntarily or not. Also, God will judge doctors who practice such procedures. *Exodus 21:22* states, *"If men strive, and hurt a woman with child, so that her fruit depart from her...he shall be surely punished..."* Some claim that a fetus is not a human, but the Bible declares, *"...thou hast covered me in my mother's womb" (Psalm 139:13).* Life starts at conception, and God covers that baby with His hand. If harm is brought to that child, both the doctor and the mother will be judged by God for committing murder. In *Jeremiah 1:5* God told Jeremiah that, *"Before I formed thee in the belly I knew thee; and before thou camest forth out of the womb I sanctified thee…"* Before we were even conceived, God knew us and had a plan for our life. Furthermore, *Psalm 22:10* says, *"…from my mother's womb you have been my God."* Isaiah 49:1-5[1] also declares that God knows us at the moment of conception and that He has a plan and purpose for each life. As Christians, we do not agree with anything that terminates life.

In short, some claim that abortion is acceptable in certain situations. One of the reasons for abortion, in my opinion, is because of lust and lust has caused society to reach all-time lows. Lust wants what is forbidden, and as a result, people have premarital sex, commit adultery, and some people even rape others to fulfill their devilish fantasies. As a result of sin and lustful desires women get pregnant, call it unexpected or unwanted and resort to abortion as a solution. The solution to pregnancy under the circumstances of premarital sex, an illicit affair or rape is adoption. Secondly, we have to deal with lust and repentance

Chapter Nine: Abortion

is mandatory if you've sinned in this area. As Christians, we must value life. It saddens me to know that millions perhaps billions of innocent children with great potential have been murdered. I pray that we always value life. Accepting abortion in any way damages our spiritual foundation.

---

[1] Listen, O isles, unto me; and hearken, ye people, from far; The LORD hath called me from the womb; from the bowels of my mother hath he made mention of my name. 2: And he hath made my mouth like a sharp sword; in the shadow of his hand hath he hid me, and made me a polished shaft; in his quiver hath he hid me; 3: And said unto me, Thou art my servant, O Israel, in whom I will be glorified. 4: Then I said, I have laboured in vain, I have spent my strength for nought, and in vain: yet surely my judgment is with the LORD, and my work with my God. 5: And now, saith the LORD that formed me from the womb to be his servant, to bring Jacob again to him, Though Israel be not gathered, yet shall I be glorious in the eyes of the LORD, and my God shall be my strength (Isaiah 49:1-5).

Chapter Ten: The Death Penalty

In this section, we have focused on the importance of preserving life; however what about the death penalty? As mentioned, life ought to be valued because when we die eternity awaits. Life is valuable, and it is worth a lot. Nevertheless, as Christians do we agree or disagree with the death penalty? Let us analyze it from a Biblical perspective.

1. **The death penalty in the Old Testament:** Throughout the Old Testament, the death penalty was pertinent for murder, kidnapping, bestiality, adultery, homosexuality, false prophets, prostitution and rape *(Exodus 21:12, 16; 22:19[1], Leviticus 20:10, 13[2] and Deuteronomy 13:5; 22:24[3])*. Although these laws were pertinent, God was occasionally merciful. For instance, David should have been executed because he was a murderer and an adulterer, but he obtained mercy *(2nd Samuel 11:1-17[4], 2nd Samuel 12:1-13[5] and Psalm 51:10-12[6])*.

2. **The death penalty in the New Testament:** Capital punishment was an established law; however, in the New Testament Jesus begins preaching and teaching new customs. He preaches peace, mercy, and forgiveness. For instance, in *John 8:1-11[7],* the woman who was caught in

Chapter Ten: The Death Penalty

adultery should have been executed, but Jesus had compassion, set her free and told her to stop sinning. Jesus excused this woman, but does that mean capital punishment is abolished? *Genesis 9:6 says, "Whoso sheddeth man's blood, by man shall his blood be shed: for in the image of God made he man."* There is an old saying, "if you do the crime you must do time." Those who commit crimes are guilty and must pay for their actions. God established capital punishment, but He is also merciful. I am not suggesting that criminals are set free from prison, but I am suggesting that we view this matter in a different light.

3. **The price of a soul:** Viewing this topic differently requires us to understand the heart of God. God does not want anyone to be lost for eternity *(2nd Peter 3:9[8])*. Yes, people are guilty if they commit a crime, but if a sinner is put to death, they will be lost forever in hell. Some state that those who have committed certain crimes should be lost in eternity, but people who say this do not understand the concept of eternal fire. One soul in hell is heartbreaking, and no one deserves to be lost. It is understandable that people want justice to be severed and

severed it must be, but if we can look at someone the way Jesus does we will never think or act the same way again.

In short, I encourage people to focus on the fact that we have eternal souls. We do not justify crimes, but life imprisonment if necessary is sufficient, but to execute judgment on someone who is not ready to meet God is incorrect. Even if someone is prepared to meet God, we ought to be compassionate. Yes, God established capital punishment, but He also established mercy and grace. Moreover, He wants everyone to inherit eternal life. Thus we must strive to help those in prison come to know whom Jesus is.

---

[1] He that smiteth a man, so that he die, shall be surely put to death. 16: And he that stealeth a man, and selleth him, or if he be found in his hand, he shall surely be put to death. 22:19: Whosoever lieth with a beast shall surely be put to death (Exodus 21:12, 16; 22:19).

[2] And the man that committeth adultery with another man's wife, even he that committeth adultery with his neighbour's wife, the adulterer and the adulteress shall surely be put to death. 13: If a man also lie with mankind, as he lieth with a woman, both of them have committed an abomination: they shall surely be put to death; their blood shall be upon them (Leviticus 20:10, 13).

Chapter Ten: The Death Penalty

---

³ And that prophet, or that dreamer of dreams, shall be put to death; because he hath spoken to turn you away from the LORD your God, which brought you out of the land of Egypt, and redeemed you out of the house of bondage, to thrust thee out of the way which the LORD thy God commanded thee to walk in. So shalt thou put the evil away from the midst of thee. 22:24: Then ye shall bring them both out unto the gate of that city, and ye shall stone them with stones that they die; the damsel, because she cried not, being in the city; and the man, because he hath humbled his neighbour's wife: so thou shalt put away evil from among you (Deuteronomy 13:5; 22:24).

⁴ 2: …David arose from off his bed, and walked upon the roof of the king's house: and from the roof he saw a woman washing herself; and the woman was very beautiful to look upon. 3: And David sent…4…messengers, and took her; and she came in unto him, and he lay with her…14…And it came to pass in the morning, that David wrote a letter to Joab, and sent it by the hand of Uriah. 15: And he wrote in the letter, saying, Set ye Uriah in the forefront of the hottest battle, and retire ye from him, that he may be smitten, and die. 16: And it came to pass, when Joab observed the city, that he assigned Uriah unto a place where he knew that valiant men were. 17: And the men of the city went out, and fought with Joab: and there fell some of the people of the servants of David; and Uriah the Hittite died also (2nd Samuel 11:2, 3, 4, 15-17).

⁵ 9…thou hast killed Uriah the Hittite with the sword, and hast taken his wife to be thy wife, and hast slain him with the sword of the children of Ammon. 13: And David said unto Nathan, I have sinned against the LORD. And Nathan said unto David, The LORD also hath put away thy sin; thou shalt not die (2nd Samuel 12:9, 12).

⁶ Create in me a clean heart, O God; and renew a right spirit within me. 11: Cast me not away from thy presence; and take not thy holy spirit from me. 12: Restore unto me the joy of thy salvation; and uphold me with thy free spirit (Psalms 51:10-12).

Understanding the Scriptures

[7] 3: And the scribes and Pharisees brought unto him a woman taken in adultery; and when they had set her in the midst, 4: They say unto him, Master, this woman was taken in adultery, in the very act. 5: Now Moses in the law commanded us, that such should be stoned: but what sayest thou? 7…He that is without sin among you, let him first cast a stone at her. 10: When Jesus had lifted up himself, and saw none but the woman, he said unto her, Woman, where are those thine accusers? hath no man condemned thee? 11: She said, No man, Lord. And Jesus said unto her, Neither do I condemn thee: go, and sin no more (John 8:3-5, 7, 10-11).

[8] The Lord is not slack concerning his promise, as some men count slackness; but is longsuffering to us-ward, not willing that any should perish, but that all should come to repentance (2nd Peter 3:9).

Chapter Eleven: War or Peace

If it be possible, as much as lieth in you, live peaceably with all men (Romans 12:18).

From whence come wars and fightings among you? come they not hence, even of your lusts that war in your members (James 4:1).

The final chapter of this section focuses on war and peace. As Christians, we do not promote violence nor should we tolerate it. We are to be peacemakers, and we are to do good unto those who persecute us *(Matthew 5:9[1] and Romans 12:20[2])*. If we are not a peacemaker, there will be confusion, which in due course will lead to wars and sequentially death. Wars are fought daily on the battlefield, in homes, in churches, and so on as battles can be either verbal or physical animosity. Our lustful desires cause wars. Lustful desires are not always sexual emotions, but can also be negative emotions which cause people to rebel, thus causing some conflict. As Christians, we must seek to follow peace with all men.

Understanding the Scriptures

1. **The battlefield:** In *Matthew 26:52[3],* Jesus was captured by His enemies and Peter tried to kill the opposing soldiers, but Jesus told him to put the weapon away. *Luke 3:14[4]* also says that we are not to be violent, hence war was never in God's plans, but because of sin there are great catastrophes and *Matthew 24:6[5]* declares that in the last days there will be wars. Nonetheless, as Christians, we need to try our best to promote peace.

2. **Wars in homes:** There are numerous dysfunctional families. *Micah 7:6* states, *"For the son dishonoureth the father, the daughter riseth up against her mother, the daughter in law against her mother in law; a man's enemies are the men of his own house."* Why are there so many problems within the home? God instituted the system of discipline and structure, but when there is no discipline or structure, it causes either verbal or physical animosity. I do not agree with abuse, but correction is appropriate when needed. Nowadays we take cues from society and no longer allow God to govern our homes, and as a result, there are problems. Disagreements are normal, and views and beliefs vary, but at the end of the

day when discipline and structure are removed, it is a recipe for trouble.

3. **Wars in churches:** As the body of Christ we are to be one. However, wars are fought in the church because of jealousy, hate, dislike, un-forgiveness, etc. As Christians, we do not approve of sin, and we adhere to a standard. Notwithstanding, we are all human, and we will make mistakes. It is, therefore, necessary that we try our best to, "...*live peaceably with all men (Romans 12:18)*. Hence, I need to ensure my spiritual wellbeing by striving to be at peace with everyone. There will always be someone who will have a problem with you, but at the end of the day, if you do not fuel the fire, it won't burn.

In short, as Christians, we are to be peacemakers and not troublemakers. The book of *Romans* tells us to try our best to live peaceably with all men. If we fail to be at peace with others, our foundation is faulty; in fact, you do not have a foundation if you are not a peacemaker. This means you can be compared to the foolish man as described in chapter one.

Understanding the Scriptures

---

[1] Blessed are the peacemakers: for they shall be called the children of God (Matthew 5:9).

[2] Therefore if thine enemy hunger, feed him; if he thirst, give him drink… (Romans 12:20).

[3] Then said Jesus unto him, Put up again thy sword into his place: for all they that take the sword shall perish with the sword (Matthew 26:52).

[4] And the soldiers likewise demanded of him, saying, And what shall we do? And he said unto them, Do violence to no man, neither accuse any falsely; and be content with your wages (Luke 3:14).

[5] And ye shall hear of wars and rumours of wars: see that ye be not troubled: for all these things must come to pass, but the end is not yet (Matthew 24:6).

Section Four: The Importance of Holiness

Abstract of section

In the previous section, we focused on ethical issues to establish a solid foundation. In this section, we will concentrate on the doctrinal matters of holiness. It is vital for Christians to answer the following questions:

- Is it mandatory for Christians to have a specific standard?
- Is holiness important?

Holiness is essential and as believers, if we follow the traditions and customs of the world, then we are of the world, and not built upon the solid Rock. The following section analyzes holiness, and this study will help believers realize that there is a need for a difference.

Chapter Twelve	The Fruit of the Spirit
Chapter Thirteen	Clothing
Chapter Fourteen	Apparel
Chapter Fifteen	Coverings
Chapter Sixteen	The Results of Unholy Living

Chapter Twelve: The Fruit of the Spirit

Galatians 5:22-23: "But the fruit of the Spirit is love, joy, peace, longsuffering, gentleness, goodness, faith, 23: Meekness, temperance..."

Holiness starts inwardly when we receive the Holy Ghost. Without the Holy Ghost, living holy is impossible. Without holiness, we cannot be saved *(Hebrews 12:14)*. Out of the heart comes good and evil, holy living and unholy living *(Matthew 12:35[1])*. Holiness is necessary, and it is sound doctrine. People often dispute holiness, but we cannot deal with the outward man until we deal with the inward man. The first sign of receiving the Holy Ghost is speaking in tongues *(Acts 2:1-4, 38-39)*. When we receive the Holy Ghost, it purifies us and teaches us so that we can distinguish between right and wrong. As the Holy Ghost works within us, God helps us to produce one fruit with nine verities or qualities which are:

1. **Love:** Primarily, we are not to love the world *(1st John 2:15)*. Secondly, we are to love everyone even our enemies *(Luke 6:27[2])*. When we receive the Holy Spirit God teaches us how to love others. *Ephesians 4:32* says,

Chapter Twelve: The Fruit of the Spirit

"And be ye kind one to another, tenderhearted, forgiving one another, even as God for Christ's sake hath forgiven you." We need to love as God loves. How can we love God who we have never seen and hate those we see *(1st John 4:20³)*. Some people dislike others; however, there is no difference between dislike and hate. If you truly have the Holy Spirit, despite your disagreements with others, you will love them, pray for them, etc.

2. **Joy:** The Bible declares that the joy of the Lord is our strength *(Nehemiah 8:10⁴)*. As Christians, we need to be joyful despite circumstances. Not everything in life will go the way we want it to go, but God always gives joy during trials.

3. **Peace:** As stated in chapter eleven, we are to be peacemakers. The beatitudes declare that peacemakers are blessed *(Matthew 5:9)*. Peace is also an inward feeling. Nowadays people try to find peace in pills, alcohol, drugs, etc. Real peace comes from God.

4. **Longsuffering:** Christ has this quality and we ought to be like Him *(2nd Peter 3:9)*. Often we are not patient, but as the Holy Ghost works within us, we will learn patience.

5. **Gentleness:** As Christians, we need to be gentle. This

does not mean we will compromise our beliefs; rather it means that we will be kind-hearted and respectful.

6. **Goodness:** Being good is a simple thing. For instance, it can be as simple as holding a door open for someone. As Christians, we need to try our best to be good towards God and people.
7. **Faith:** Numerous books have been written on faith, but as Christians, if we have the spirit within us, it must produce the virtue of faith.
8. **Meekness:** According to Webster's Dictionary, *"the absence of any feelings of being better than others."* Being meek is being humble.
9. **Temperance:** This means being self-disciplined, and as Christians, this is a necessity.

In short, all of the qualities of the fruit of the spirit come through the Holy Ghost. If we do not have these qualities, then it is doubtful that we have the Holy Ghost because if we have God's spirit, then we ought to have His attributes. *John 15:1-6*[5] says that those who do not produce fruit shall be cast into the fire. We must have the qualities mentioned in this chapter, and once we do, the outward man

Chapter Twelve: The Fruit of the Spirit

will begin to change because God desires outward changes as well.

---

[1] A good man out of the good treasure of the heart bringeth forth good things: and an evil man out of the evil treasure bringeth forth evil things (Matthew 12:35).

[2] ... Love your enemies, do good to them which hate you (Luke 6:27).

[3] If a man say, I love God, and hateth his brother, he is a liar: for he that loveth not his brother whom he hath seen, how can he love God whom he hath not seen (1st John 4:20).

[4] ...the joy of the LORD is your strength (Nehemiah 8:10).

[5] I am the true vine, and my Father is the husbandman. 2: Every branch in me that beareth not fruit he taketh away: and every *branch* that beareth fruit, he purgeth it, that it may bring forth more fruit. 3: Now ye are clean through the word which I have spoken unto you. 4: Abide in me, and I in you. As the branch cannot bear fruit of itself, except it abide in the vine; no more can ye, except ye abide in me. 5: I am the vine, ye *are* the branches: He that abideth in me, and I in him, the same bringeth forth much fruit: for without me ye can do nothing. 6: If a man abide not in me, he is cast forth as a branch, and is withered; and men gather them, and cast *them* into the fire, and they are burned (John 15:1-6).

Chapter Thirteen: Clothing

*The woman shall not wear that which pertaineth unto a man, neither shall a man put on a woman's garment: for all that do so are **abomination** unto the LORD thy God (Deuteronomy 22:5).*

Many assume they can dress as they please, but it was never like that in the Bible days nor should it be like that today. Garments are to be gender-specific, and there must be a very distinct, clear and visible difference between the children of God and the children of the devil. The clothing of a Christian should be unquestionable, decent and modest because a child of God should look like a child of God. According to God's Word, outward appearance is important. The issue of clothing is a critical subject because cross-dressing is an abominable act and *Revelation 21:27*[1] says that those who commit abominable acts cannot go to heaven. Some say that *Deuteronomy 22:5* cannot be used to preach against cross-dressing and note that there are other regulations in that chapter that we must follow if we want to teach against cross-dressing. If you study that chapter carefully verse 5 is the only verse in that chapter that refers

Chapter Thirteen: Clothing

to an abominable act. Therefore, we must not compromise and preach against cross-dressing.

The Bible does not specify in detail a general standard for men or women, but as God's temple, we are not to defile our bodies *(1st Corinthians 6:19[2])*. Immodest clothing draws attention and causes lust. *Matthew 5:28[3]* says those who lust in their hearts commit adultery. Also, an immodestly dressed person is guilty of helping onlookers commit adultery; consequently judgment will fall upon both parties as stated in *Romans 14:13[4]*. According to Harris (2003), men and women are different when it comes to lust in that, *"...men are tempted by the pleasure lust offers, while women are tempted by the power lust promises."* Lust drives men because they find physical pleasure in them. Women, on the other hand, are concerned about emotional pleasure. Men are attracted by sight and women know this; thus they often exploit themselves to fulfill their emotional desires. Harris goes on to state some specifics about women, *"...when you wear clothing that accentuates, draws attention to, or highlights the feminine parts of your body...and behave in a way that is designed primarily to arouse sexual desire in men, you're committing pornography with your life"* (p. 87, 91-92).

Understanding the Scriptures

When women dress immodestly or when men play on women's emotions it's wrong. It is therefore vital that there is a standard of holiness because, without a standard for men and women, it will bring about immodest actions and can cause others to fall.

I recommend the following standard, and I believe that this is based on biblical principles. (Please note that this recommendation is based on North American culture and may not be applicable in other parts of the world. Nevertheless, garments should be gender specific, and anything that causes lust should be avoided).

Standard for women

Modest dress (skirts that pass the knees while sitting with no splits as well as no revealing clothing that exposes cleavage, underarms or any other body parts). In regards to sporting activities or the gym, maintaining a godly standard is crucial. (*Deuteronomy 22:5, I Corinthians 6:19, Revelation 21:27* and *Luke 17:1-2^5*).

Chapter Thirteen: Clothing

Standard for men

Modest dress (neatly dressed in pants and shirt. While in church dressed neatly in shirt and tie. While outside of church no baggy pants because this reflects the image of worldliness. Furthermore, men's shirts should not expose any part of their body.) In regards to sporting activities or the gym it is essential to maintain a godly standard and that whatever we wear is not contrary to the teachings of the Bible *(Deuteronomy 22:5, I Corinthians 6:19, Revelation 21:27* and *Luke 17:1-2*

To conclude, some people may state that these are man-made rules, but it is important to realize that the Bible encourages us to present our bodies as a living sacrifice and this is the perfect and acceptable will of God *(Romans 12:1-2)*. When we defy God's Word and dress or do as we please, lust builds within our system and eventually will destroy us. It is vital that our dress code whether visible or not does not cause lust. For instance, perfume or cologne is often used to enhance one's smell. Certain perfumes and colognes have a sexual connotation and create lustful thoughts or lead to lustful actions. Using perfume or cologne is not wrong, but if what we do cause others to stumble and fall it is wrong.

Causing temptation is dangerous and leads to the lake of fire. However, it is also important to note that modesty does not prevent lusters from being attracted to you. Nevertheless, that does not eliminate the standards. As mentioned, there must be a distinct, clear and visible difference between the children of God and the children of the devil. The foundation of a home should be stable; likewise, our spiritual foundation should be firm. Thus, if we remain unclear, we will eventually go with the flow and overtime our foundation will fail and ultimately be destroyed.

---

[1] And there shall in no wise enter into it any thing that defileth, neither *whatsoever* worketh abomination… (Revelation 21:27).

[2] What? know ye not that your body is the temple of the Holy Ghost *which is* in you, which ye have of God, and ye are not your own (1st Corinthians 6:19)

[3] …whosoever looketh on a woman to lust after her hath committed adultery with her already in his heart (Matthew 5:28).

[4] Let us not therefore judge one another any more: but judge this rather, that no man put a stumblingblock or an occasion to fall in *his* brother's way (Romans 14:13).

[5] …offences will come: but woe *unto him,* through whom they come! 2: It were better for him that a millstone were hanged about his neck, and he cast into the sea, than that he should offend one of these little ones (Luke 17:1-2).

Chapter Fourteen: Apparel

"In like manner also, that women adorn themselves in modest apparel, with shamefacedness and sobriety; not with broided hair, or gold, or pearls, or costly array" (1st Timothy 2:9).

Some individuals state that the above verse has nothing to do with holiness; however, this is a fallacy. There are several things mentioned in the above reference that depicts holiness, and they are analyzed as follows:

1. **Shamefacedness:** The New Testament Greek lexicon refers to this as *"Aidōs"* which is, *"a sense of shame or honour, modesty, bashfulness, reverence, regard for others, respect."* Many feel ashamed of themselves when in their natural state, therefore they use makeup. There are different types of makeup, but all types are inappropriate. According to Pack (2008), makeup started in Egypt, and numerous pagans such as the Assyrians and Persians used makeup for various purposes. He also states that the first women to wear makeup were prostitutes. They changed their natural appearance in an attempt to cause men to

commit adultery. *Proverbs 6:25* says, *"Lust not after her beauty in thine heart; neither let her take thee with her eyelids."* The previous verse is referring to women who use makeup to cause men to lust, and a warning is given to men to be careful. Makeup has always been used by women and even men for sexual purposes. It represents boldness, seduction, ostentation, and prostitution. Women and men should not use makeup as it is a direct act of rebellion towards God and it suggests that God did not do a good job. Some people try to validate the use of makeup and state that using it for a special event or employment purposes is appropriate. Trying to approve what God has outlawed is irrational. The Bible discourages makeup as seen in *Jeremiah 4:30*[1] and *Ezekiel 23:40, 44*[2].

2. **Broided hair:** According to the New Testament Greek lexicon it means woven (weaving), plaited (plaiting, braiding, weaving, stitching or twisting together your hair). In the Bible days, it was a hairstyle that involved braided hair with gold or pearls in it. It is not speaking of merely braiding your hair as some suggest. Women in that time would often immodestly braid their hair weaving expensive jewelry into it. Nowadays broided hair is

Chapter Fourteen: Apparel

similar to the practices of old, but added elements such as weaves, plaiting and so forth are common. The Bible encourages women to avoid doing this. A woman's hair is her glory, and when the natural appearance of anything is changed, it suggests that God did not do a good job. In the next chapter, you will read about coverings, but it is important to note that your hair should always be in its natural state.

3. **The wearing of jewelry:** *1st Timothy 2:9* discourage the wearing of jewelry. The Bible notes, *"Your beauty should not come from outward adornment, such as braided hair and the wearing of gold jewelry and fine clothes. 4: Instead, it should be that of your inner self, the unfading beauty of a gentle and quiet spirit, which is of great worth in God's sight" (1st Peter 3:3-4 NLT).* Some say inner holiness is what matters. God desires inner holiness, but He also wants that inward holiness is manifest on the outside without the adornment of jewelry. Here are some important notes regarding this issue.

- **So-called contradictions regarding jewelry:** Some people try to find inconsistencies in the Bible concerning this issue and several verses in the Bible seem to encourage the wearing of jewelry such as, *Genesis 24:47-48; 35:1-4; 41:41-42³, Ezekiel 16:11-13, 15-20⁴, and Luke 15:22⁵, etc.* In each of the references jewelry was used for a particular purpose such as the declaration of son-ship or kingship, however, jewelry was disposed of, or those who wore it became vile and sinned. God never intended for us to wear jewelry, especially His chosen people.

- **Jewelry is forbidden:** God forbids the wearing of jewelry, and it is an abomination according to *Deuteronomy 7:25, "...thou shalt not desire the silver or gold that is on them, nor take it unto thee...for it is an **abomination** to the LORD thy God."* The Israelites were told that they should not desire the jewels of the Egyptians because it was abdominal. Similarly Christians today should not desire any jewels as jewelry throughout history has always been connected to Egypt, which is a type of sin and bondage.

- **Jewelry causes pride:** People who wear jewelry are proud of what they have. The devil was proud of the jewels he had because it caused the angles in heaven to worship the image of God that was seen in his jewels,

Chapter Fourteen: Apparel

consequently causing pride and his downfall *(Ezekiel 28:11-17[6])*. When a person gets a new ring or earrings, they tend to show it off, and this is pride. *Proverbs 16:18 says, "Pride goeth before destruction, and an haughty spirit before a fall."*

- **Judgment for using jewelry:** In the Old Testament when people used jewelry they were rebuked. For instance, when the children of Israel made the golden calf God rebuked them through Moses *(Exodus 33:4-6[7])*. Likewise, if we use what is forbidden judgment is a must.

- **Change and jewelry in the Old Testament:** When someone is filled with God's spirit, inward changes happen, and these changes are made manifest on the outside. As Christians, we should not even own jewelry. In fact, in the Old Testament, the children of Israel did not own any jewelry because everything they had was borrowed *(Exodus 11:2[8])*. In *Exodus 35:22[9]*, the Israelites offered jewelry for the construction of the tabernacle, and this was excess from what they had borrowed. All the jewelry they acquired was intended for specific purposes. As Christians, we need to be unique and different because God's children have always been distinct. For instance, the children of Israel were not permitted to cut the corners of their fields when it was harvest time *(Leviticus 19:9-10[10])*. This act of obedience proved that they were children of God. Christians who do not wear jewelry show that they are God's representatives.

- **Appropriate versus Inappropriate:** Based on the analysis completed, it is safe to conclude that wearing jewelry is wrong; however some types of jewelry such as wristwatches, medical bracelets, and wedding rings need to be analyzed to determine if these types of jewelry have a practical purpose or not. If what you are wearing does not serve a practical purpose you should not use it. We shall analyze these three types of jewelry below:

1. **Wristwatches:** A wristwatch is used to keep track of time. As Christians, we should be on time and having a watch helps. However, if a person has a personal conviction, he/she should not use one. (Please note that personal convictions should not be set as church standards). If you decide to use one, your wristwatch should be modest and not

Chapter Fourteen: Apparel

be a center of attraction.

2. **Medical bracelets:** Medical bracelets also serve a practical purpose of altering others about medical conditions. This helps to avoid inappropriate medical treatment in the event of an emergency. Again if you decide to use one, your medical bracelet should be modest and decent. It must not be a center of attraction.

3. **Wedding Rings:** Wedding rings are used to represent marital status. Some believe wedding rings have a practical purpose while others disagree. According to Bernard (1985), *"...in some cultures failure to wear the wedding ring can imply that one is living in fornication, thereby creating a possible stumbling block for an observer." (p. 105)*. He also states, *"rings are undoubtedly a form of jewelry." (p. 178)*. The Bible says that we should not wear gold and this includes rings of all types. According to Bacchiocchi (1997), wedding rings appear to have originated in Egypt and were a sign of bondage. He also states that exchanging rings originated from pagan customs. Furthermore, rings were used to tell fortunes and represented idolatry. Carmela (2005), agrees that wedding rings originated in Egypt. She notes that Egyptians believed they discovered a vein that ran

from the finger straight to the heart. Firstly, the Bible tells us that our hearts are wicked *(Jeremiah 17:9[11])*. Secondly, Egypt is a type of sin and bondage. Wedding rings are indeed jewelry, and to some, they do not serve a practical purpose because of the connection to everything that represents sin. To others, wedding rings are significant. I do not believe it is mandatory to wear one, but I have also concluded that wearing one is a personal choice. Like the other two points, I recommend wedding rings to be modest and decent. It must not be a center of attraction nor should someone wear it if God places a conviction in their heart. Those who do not wear rings may ask, "How will people know I am married without a ring, what if it implies that I am living in sin or what if it's a stumbling block to others?" Marriage is represented by a couples actions and not by the symbol upon their finger. Everyone has a purpose for using or not using a wedding ring. In short, this issue is one that requires personal prayer and conviction.

Conclusively, God has called us, and as His chosen people we must not adorn ourselves with jewelry. If we use earrings, rings, tie clips, brooches, cuff links, plastic jewelry and other types of jewelry, we have compromised the

Chapter Fourteen: Apparel

standard of God because the Bible tells us that we ought not to wear jewelry, and the above mentioned is adornment. If we disobey or compromise the standard of God in the slightest way, our foundation will be jeopardized.

---

[1] And *when* thou *art* spoiled, what wilt thou do? Though thou clothest thyself with crimson, though thou deckest thee with ornaments of gold, though **thou rentest thy face with painting,** in vain shalt thou make thyself fair; *thy* lovers will despise thee, they will seek thy life (Jeremiah 4:30).

[2] And furthermore, that ye have sent for men to come from far, unto whom a messenger *was* sent; and, lo, they came: for whom thou didst wash thyself, paintedst thy eyes, and deckedst thyself with ornaments...44: a woman that playeth the harlot... (Ezekiel 23:40, 44).

[3] And I asked her, and said, Whose daughter *art* thou? And she said, The daughter of Bethuel, Nahor's son, whom Milcah bare unto him: and I put the earring upon her face, and the bracelets upon her hands. 48: And I bowed down my head, and worshipped the LORD, and blessed the LORD God of my master Abraham, which had led me in the right way to take my master's brother's daughter unto his son. 35:1: And God said unto Jacob, Arise, go up to Bethel, and dwell there: and make there an altar unto God, that appeared unto thee when thou fleddest from the face of Esau thy brother. 35:2: Then Jacob said unto his household, and to all that *were* with him, Put away the strange gods that *are* among you, and be clean, and change your garments: 35:3: And let us arise, and go up to Bethel; and I will make there an altar unto God, who answered me in the day of my distress, and was with me in the way which I went. 35:4: And they gave unto Jacob all the strange gods which *were* in their hand, and *all their* earrings which *were* in their ears; and Jacob hid them under the oak

which *was* by Shechem. 41:41: And Pharaoh said unto Joseph, See, I have set thee over all the land of Egypt. 41:42 And Pharaoh took off his ring from his hand, and put it upon Joseph's hand, and arrayed him in vestures of fine linen, and put a gold chain about his neck (Genesis 24:47-48; 35:1-4; 41:41-42).

[4] I decked thee also with ornaments, and I put bracelets upon thy hands, and a chain on thy neck. 12: And I put a jewel on thy forehead, and earrings in thine ears, and a beautiful crown upon thine head. 13: Thus wast thou decked with gold and silver; and thy raiment *was of* fine linen, and silk, and broidered work; thou didst eat fine flour, and honey, and oil: and thou wast exceeding beautiful, and thou didst prosper into a kingdom. 15: But thou didst trust in thine own beauty, and playedst the harlot because of thy renown, and pouredst out thy fornications on every one that passed by; his it was. 16: And of thy garments thou didst take, and deckedst thy high places with divers colours, and playedst the harlot thereupon: *the like things* shall not come, neither shall it be *so*. 17: Thou hast also taken thy fair jewels of my gold and of my silver, which I had given thee, and madest to thyself images of men, and didst commit whoredom with them, 18: And tookest thy broidered garments, and coveredst them: and thou hast set mine oil and mine incense before them. 19: My meat also which I gave thee, fine flour, and oil, and honey, *wherewith* I fed thee, thou hast even set it before them for a sweet savour: and *thus* it was, saith the Lord GOD. 20: Moreover thou hast taken thy sons and thy daughters, whom thou hast borne unto me, and these hast thou sacrificed unto them to be devoured. *Is this* of thy whoredoms a small matter (Ezekiel 16:11-13, 15-20).

[5] But the father said to his servants, Bring forth the best robe, and put *it* on him; and put a ring on his hand, and shoes on *his* feet (Luke 15:22).

[6] Moreover the word of the LORD came unto me, saying, 12: Son of man, take up a lamentation upon the king of Tyrus, and say unto him, Thus saith the Lord GOD;

Chapter Fourteen: Apparel

Thou sealest up the sum, full of wisdom, and perfect in beauty. 13: Thou hast been in Eden the garden of God; every precious stone *was* thy covering, the sardius, topaz, and the diamond, the beryl, the onyx, and the jasper, the sapphire, the emerald, and the carbuncle, and gold: the workmanship of thy tabrets and of thy pipes was prepared in thee in the day that thou wast created. 14: Thou *art* the anointed cherub that covereth; and I have set thee *so:* thou wast upon the holy mountain of God; thou hast walked up and down in the midst of the stones of fire. 15: Thou *wast* perfect in thy ways from the day that thou wast created, till iniquity was found in thee. 16: By the multitude of thy merchandise they have filled the midst of thee with violence, and thou hast sinned: therefore I will cast thee as profane out of the mountain of God: and I will destroy thee, O covering cherub, from the midst of the stones of fire. 17: Thine heart was lifted up because of thy beauty, thou hast corrupted thy wisdom by reason of thy brightness: I will cast thee to the ground, I will lay thee before kings, that they may behold thee (Ezekiel 28:11-17).

[7] And when the people heard these evil tidings, they mourned: and no man did put on him his ornaments. 5: For the LORD had said unto Moses, Say unto the children of Israel, Ye *are* a stiffnecked people: I will come up into the midst of thee in a moment, and consume thee: therefore now put off thy ornaments from thee, that I may know what to do unto thee. 6: And the children of Israel stripped themselves of their ornaments by the mount Horeb (Exodus 33:4-6).

[8] Speak now in the ears of the people, and let every man borrow of his neighbour, and every woman of her neighbour, jewels of silver, and jewels of gold (Exodus 11:2).

[9] And they came, both men and women, as many as were willing hearted, *and* brought bracelets, and earrings, and rings, and tablets, all jewels of gold: and every man that offered *offered* an offering of gold unto the LORD (Exodus 35:22).

Understanding the Scriptures

---

[10] And when ye reap the harvest of your land, thou shalt not wholly reap the corners of thy field, neither shalt thou gather the gleanings of thy harvest. 10: And thou shalt not glean thy vineyard, neither shalt thou gather *every* grape of thy vineyard; thou shalt leave them for the poor and stranger: I *am* the LORD your God (Leviticus 19:9-10).

[11] The heart *is* deceitful above all *things,* and desperately wicked: who can know it (Jeremiah 17:9).

Chapter Fifteen: Coverings

Many people cannot comprehend coverings and 1st Corinthians 11:3-15, is an intense passage of discussion among believers. There are three coverings talked about in this passage, which are the spiritual covering, the temporal covering (a hat or a veil) and the physical covering (a person's hair). Obedience in all three of these areas brings the blessing of God, and all three coverings are essential, therefore let's analyze these according to the Word. It is essential to understand that this standard applies to those who are single and married.

1. **The spiritual covering:** *1st Corinthians 11:3* refers to the spiritual covering, *"But I would have you know, that the head of every man is Christ; and the head of the woman is the man; and the head of Christ is God."* This verse notes that:
- **Christ is the head of the man:** When we obey the gospel, we inherit salvation, which in turn covers us spiritually. To be covered, we had to obey the Word of God. If we disobey His Word we uncover ourselves, and the Bible says, *"...he will pour out his anger and wrath on those who...refuse to obey the truth"*

(Romans 2:8 NLT). Disobedience brings judgment, which means we are no longer covered spiritually whereas obedience covers us and protects us.

- **The head of the woman is the man:** This does not make men authoritarians because husbands must respect their wives, if not their prayers will be hindered *(1st Peter 3:7[1])*. Husbands must love their wives as Christ loved the church *(Ephesians 5:25[2])* and Christ loved the church sacrificially, therefore when a husband obeys these verses they are covered spiritually.
- **Women**: Women are covered spiritually by obeying the gospel and by respecting their husbands *(Ephesians 5:22[3])*.
- **God is the head of Christ:** Obedience covers us spiritually. Jesus was covered spiritually because He was obedient even unto death as stated in *Philippians 2:8[4]*.

2. **The temporal covering**: The temporal covering (a hat or a veil) is common in many cultures. The temporary covering is a subject of great confusion. To understand this issue each verse from *1st Corinthians 11*, referring to

Chapter Fifteen: Coverings

the temporal covering will be analyzed.

- According to *1st Corinthians 11:4,* men do not cover their head. *"Every man praying or prophesying, having his head covered, dishonoureth his head."* When a man prays with his head covered he dishonors his head, which is Christ.

- *1st Corinthians 11:5* gives the reason why women ought to cover their head with a veil or a hat. *"But every woman who has her head uncovered while praying or prophesying disgraces her head, for she is one and the same as the woman whose head is shaved" (New American Standard Bible).* According to this verse, it is a disgrace for a woman to pray or prophesy unveiled. Women who pray unveiled dishonor their husband and Christ.

- *"If a woman does not cover her head, she should have her hair cut off; and if it is a disgrace for a woman to have her hair cut or shaved off, she should cover her head"(1st Corinthians 11:6 NLT).* Here, Paul tells us that if a woman refuses to cover her head, she should cut off all her hair. He then states that it is shameful for women to cut all their hair or to be bald; therefore women should wear a head covering.

- *1st Corinthians 11:7&10* focuses on men, the temporary covering and why women should use one. *"A man should not wear anything on his head when worshiping, for man is made in God's image and reflects God's glory. And woman reflects man's glory 10: For this reason, and because the angels are watching, a woman should wear a covering on her head to show she is under authority"* (NLT). Men do not cover their head because it dishonors God, but women should wear a veil or a hat while praying or prophesying because it is a sign of respect towards her husband and the Bible says that the angels are watching when women cover their heads.

- *1st Corinthians 11:13* then asks a question, *"Judge for yourselves. Is it right for a woman to pray to God in public without covering her head"* (NLT). The answer to this question is no. Some churches believe that the second covering is not necessary; others think it's always needed, while others believe it's only required if women will pray, prophesy or be in the presence of God. Firstly, we are always in the presence of God.

Chapter Fifteen: Coverings

Secondly, praying and prophesying can be done anywhere. A covering is only necessary while in church because the word public is referring to public worship as described in the Good New Version of the Bible. Often public worship is done at church. There is no indication that God will not answer a woman who is not veiled while in church or that she will go to hell. Furthermore, some ask if a covering is necessary while praying at home, in the hospital, etc. Women are only obliged to cover their head while in church because it is a sign of respect toward her husband and God. I encourage a covering in all settings if it is possible. If not possible as mentioned in regards to the other situations, a covering is not mandatory because the individual is covered physically.

3. **The physical covering**: The physical covering (a person's hair) is indicated in *1st Corinthians 11:14* and this verse tells us that nature teaches us that it is a shame for a man to have long hair, but a woman's long hair is her glory. Long here does not simply mean length of the hair. It means to let the hair grow. For men, it is recommended that men's hair length is low-cut. Please see diagram 1 for

recommendations. *Verse 15,* on the other hand, states that a woman's long hair (hair that is growing/uncut) is her covering and glory. Although the Bible refers to a woman's hair as a covering, it does not eliminate the second covering. Not only is a woman covered temporally, but she is also covered spiritually and physically. Women can still pray and be blessed by God without the second covering even in the church despite beliefs that may indicate otherwise. The second covering merely is a sign of respect. Nevertheless, obeying the principle of using a second covering and maintaining a feminine hairstyle indicates acceptance of a man's leadership, submission to God and your spouse. In short, all coverings mentioned herein are of importance. I recommend you watch our video lesson on this topic on YouTube at Lighthouse Tabernacle Apostolic.

In short, it is vital to understand and obey the Scriptures. Seek God and study His Word if you are uncertain about the issues presented in this chapter. All the coverings are of equal importance.

Chapter Fifteen: Coverings

Diagram 1,

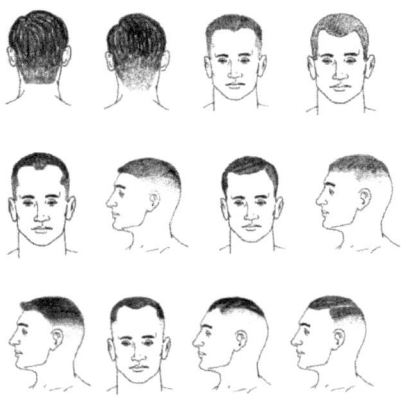

---

[1] Likewise, ye husbands, dwell with *them* according to knowledge, giving honour unto the wife, as unto the weaker vessel, and as being heirs together of the grace of life; that your prayers be not hindered (1st Peter 3:7).

[2] Husbands, love your wives, even as Christ also loved the church, and gave himself for it (Ephesians 5:25).

[3] Wives, submit yourselves unto your own husbands, as unto the Lord (Ephesians 5:22).

[4] And being found in fashion as a man, he humbled himself, and became obedient unto death, even the death of the cross (Philippians 2:8).

Chapter Sixteen: The Results of Unholy Living

Hebrews 12:14, "Follow peace with all men, and holiness, without which no man shall see the Lord."

Romans 12:1-2, "I beseech you therefore, brethren, by the mercies of God, that ye present your bodies a living sacrifice, holy, acceptable unto God, which is your reasonable service. 2: And be not conformed to this world: but be ye transformed by the renewing of your mind, that ye may prove what is that good, and acceptable, and perfect, will of God."

2nd Corinthians 6:17, "Wherefore come out from among them, and be ye separate, saith the Lord, and touch not the unclean thing; and I will receive you."

1st John 2:15, "Love not the world, neither the things that are in the world. If any man love the world, the love of the Father is not in him."

Many Biblical references encourage holy living, and if we do not adhere to what is written in the Bible, we cannot enharit eternal life. The ultimate punishment of living an

Chapter Sixteen: The Results of Unholy Living

unholy life. We must have an inward and outward standard of holiness. Within we must have the qualities of the fruit of the spirit whereas the outward man must adhere to the dress code and principles established in this book, which are based on the Bible.

Are sinners judged according to holinesses standards?

Luke 12:45-48[1] declares that those who know the will of God and do it not will have a greater judgment than those who do not know it. Sinner or saint, we are all going to be judged according to the Word of God. Ignorance of the law does not pardon one's actions. However, as Christians when working with sinners, such topics should be avoided until,

1. The person has completed a home bible study.
2. Has repented, been baptized in Jesus name and has received the Holy Ghost.
3. They have completed a discipleship program.

In short, holiness is necessary, and we need to love it because it will save us.

---

[1] But and if that servant say in his heart, My lord delayeth his coming; and shall begin

Understanding the Scriptures

to beat the menservants and maidens, and to eat and drink, and to be drunken; 46: The lord of that servant will come in a day when he looketh not for *him,* and at an hour when he is not aware, and will cut him in sunder, and will appoint him his portion with the unbelievers. 47: And that servant, which knew his lord's will, and prepared not *himself,* neither did according to his will, shall be beaten with many *stripes.* 48: But he that knew not, and did commit things worthy of stripes, shall be beaten with few *stripes.* For unto whomsoever much is given, of him shall be much required: and to whom men have committed much, of him they will ask the more (Luke 12:45-48).

Section Five: Prophecy

Abstract of section

To conclude this book we shall analyze the rapture and the tribulation after that. The purpose of having boundaries and avoiding sin is to ensure that we are prepared when the Lord comes back.

Chapter Seventeen	The Rapture & the Tribulation

Chapter Seventeen: The Rapture & Tribulation

In our analysis, three points shall be examined, and they are:

1. **Death and the rapture:** Throughout history, so-called prophets have tried to determine when the world would end; however, the Bible says, *"But of that day and hour knoweth no man, no, not the angels of heaven, but my Father only" (Matthew 24:36)*. Some declare the Lord will never come, *"...Where is the promise of his coming? for since the fathers fell asleep, all things continue as they were from the beginning of the creation (2nd Peter 3:4)*. The Bible declares that God is longsuffering because He does not want anyone to perish. Jesus wants everyone to come to repentance *(2nd Peter 3:9)*. Views and beliefs will always be an issue with regards to this subject, but of a certainty one day we will all pay the price for our sins. At creation, humanity was sinless, healthy and immortal. However, disobedience to God's commandment brought sin into the world, which causes death. So, even if you do not believe that Jesus will return, we will one day pay for our sins. Also, the Bible says, *"For the wages of sin is death..." (Romans 6:23)*. The word death in this verse is

Chapter Seventeen: The Rapture & Tribulation

referring to eternal damnation. If you fear death, it is because you know that there is more afterward. *1st John 4:18* states, *"There is no fear in love; but perfect love casteth out fear: because fear hath torment. He that feareth is not made perfect in love."* If we fear death, it is an indication that we are not right with God and that's why the thought of dying torments some. But glory to God, if we live a righteous life, we have the hope and assurance that we will reign with our Saviour forever. If a believer dies they are present with Him, however, we also know that death is temporal, and one day Jesus will return as declared in *1st Thessalonians 4:16-17*[1]. The Lord Himself will descend from heaven with a shout, the dead in Christ will rise first, and the righteous who are alive and remain will meet the Lord and the other saints in the air. *1st Corinthians 15:51-55*[2] also states that not everyone will sleep (die) and that in the twinkling of an eye we will be changed as our natural body becomes glorified. Whether dead or alive corruption will become incorruptible and mortality will become immortality. *Isaiah 26:19* states, *"Thy dead men shall live, together with my dead body shall they arise. Awake and sing, ye that dwell in dust: for thy dew is as the dew of herbs, and the earth shall cast out the dead." 1ˢᵗ John 3:2³* declares that one day we will be like Jesus. Hallelujah, praise God, what a glorious day that will be.

2. **After the rapture**: There will be a seven-year period when the Lord pours His wrath upon the earth. Some believe that the church will be here during this period while others disagree. It is important to note that we as the church are not trying to save people from the antichrist; instead, we are trying to keep people from eternal fire. *Daniel 9:27⁴* refers to the tribulation and *Revelation* chapters *6, 8,* and *16* refers to what will happen during the tribulation. (Please see appendix two for details). Before analyzing what will happen during the tribulation, it is important to note that after the rapture there will be chaos because, in one sixty-fourth of a second, millions perhaps billions of people will vanish from the face of the earth. Additionally, millions perhaps billions of graves containing the bodies of the saints will be empty. The rapture will cause fear, confusion, destruction and there will be no peace after this event. During this chaos the antichrist will be revealed, he will declare peace, will set

Chapter Seventeen: The Rapture & Tribulation

up a one-world government and will introduce the mark of the beast *(Revelation 13:1, 17-18[5]). Daniel 9:27* states, that the antichrist will make a covenant with many, which is the seven-year peace treaty with Israel. The one world government is a union of ten nations that will serve the Antichrist and rule the world. The mark of the beast will replace the failing currency, which has been happening throughout the world as of late. Furthermore, many will be deceived into taking the mark because, for the first 3½ years of the tribulation, the antichrist will pretend to be peaceful and displays great authority. During the tribulation, the antichrist will rebuild Solomon's temple as this is a clause in the peace treaty. Upon completing the temple, the antichrist will sit upon the throne and declare that he is god. When this happens, the nation of Israel will acknowledge that he is not the true Messiah and will refuse to serve him. This is when the antichrist stops the sacrifices and offerings. From this point on the tribulation will continue. Armageddon closes out the tribulation, and the Bible states that God has sealed a hundred and forty-four thousand people from the twelve tribes of Israel that will be hidden from the destruction of the antichrist at

Armageddon. Some claim that this number represents the number of people that will be in heaven; however, multitudes will be in heaven *(Revelation 7:9[6])*. Furthermore, the multitude in heaven also represents the tribulation saints as they will also be hidden from the destruction of the antichrist at Armageddon. *"...These are they which came out of great tribulation..." (Revelation 7:14)*. The Lord Himself will come down at Armageddon with His angels and will destroy the antichrist and His army *(Revelation 19:11, 14, 16[7])*.

- **After the tribulation:** Jesus Christ will reign on earth with the resurrected tribulation saints for a thousand years, and during this time the devil will be bound. After the millennium, the devil will be let loose to tempt those that reign with Christ. The devil and an innumerable army of demons will attempt to conquer the tribulation saints; however, this attack will be unsuccessful as the demons will be devoured by fire and the devil will sent to the lake of fire *(Ephesians 6:12[8], Revelation 20:7-9[9])*. Consequently, a proper analysis of *Revelation 6:11; 20:4-5[10]*, reveals the answer as to why the tribulations saints only rest for a

Chapter Seventeen: The Rapture & Tribulation

season (1000 years). They rest for a season because their enemy has not yet become their footstool. *"....The LORD said unto my Lord, Sit thou at my right hand, until I make thine enemies thy footstool" (Psalms 110:1).*

- **The final judgment:** The great white judgment throne is the next thing that will take place, and this is when the second resurrection happens. All those that died from the beginning of time will be judged. The only people who will not be judged are the saints that arose after the resurrection of Christ, the saints that were caught up and the tribulation saints who reigned with Christ for a thousand years as all these people are a part of the first resurrection. Books will judge those who stand before Christ. Those books are the Bible, the record of spoken words and the book of life *(Mark 13:31[11], Matthew 12:36[12] and Revelation 20:15[13])*. Whosoever is not found in the book of life is cast into hell and hell will be thrown into the lake of fire. The earth will be burned with fire; the New Jerusalem will come down from God out of heaven and time will be no more *(2nd Peter 3:7[14], and Revelation 21:1-2[15])*.

3. **Will the church go through the tribulation:** This is a ubiquitous question; however, the church will not go through the tribulation, and this is evident in the Scriptures.

- Firstly, before the Lord comes, there will be a great falling away (many will turn away from the truth), and then the antichrist will come into power. *"Let no man deceive you by any means: for that day shall not come, except there come a falling away first, and that man of sin be revealed, the son of perdition"* (2nd *Thessalonians 2:3).* It is apparent that many are turning from the faith; however, there is also great revival. The revival started at Pentecost when the Holy Ghost came down. *"And it shall come to pass in the last days, saith God, I will pour out of my Spirit upon all flesh..." (Acts 2:17).*

- Secondly, *Matthew 24:29,31* states that the Lord will return after the tribulation and that He will send His angels to gather the elect. *1st Thessalonians 4:16-18,* on the other hand, declares the Lord Himself comes down. These are two different events because the elect in *Thessalonians* is the church whereas the elect in

Chapter Seventeen: The Rapture & Tribulation

Matthew 24 is the hundred and forty-four thousand along with the tribulation saints who will be saved/hidden from the destruction of the antichrist at Armageddon.

In short, many verses could be analyzed; nevertheless, beyond a shadow of a doubt, we are living in the end times. The signs of times are visible. Consider the weather, wars and the tragedies of this world. All this reveals that the coming of the Lord is near. If we are not ready to meet God, we will go through the tribulation. The only way to be saved during the tribulation is by way of death. I would rather get right with God now because the road we walk on now is much easier. In the days of the antichrist, it will not be easy. If there is ever a time to be serious and build a proper foundation, the time is now.

---

[1] For the Lord himself shall descend from heaven with a shout, with the voice of the archangel, and with the trump of God: and the dead in Christ shall rise first: 17: Then we which are alive *and* remain shall be caught up together with them in the clouds, to meet the Lord in the air: and so shall we ever be with the Lord. 18: Wherefore comfort one another with these words (1st Thessalonians 4:16-18).

Understanding the Scriptures

² Behold, I shew you a mystery; We shall not all sleep, but we shall all be changed, 52: In a moment, in the twinkling of an eye, at the last trump: for the trumpet shall sound, and the dead shall be raised incorruptible, and we shall be changed. 53: For this corruptible must put on incorruption, and this mortal *must* put on immortality. 54: So when this corruptible shall have put on incorruption, and this mortal shall have put on immortality, then shall be brought to pass the saying that is written, Death is swallowed up in victory. 55: O death, where *is* thy sting? O grave, where *is* thy victory (1ˢᵗ Corinthians 15:51-55).

³ Beloved, now are we the sons of God, and it doth not yet appear what we shall be: but we know that, when he shall appear, we shall be like him; for we shall see him as he is (1ˢᵗ John 3:2).

⁴ And he shall confirm the covenant with many for one week: and in the midst of the week he shall cause the sacrifice and the oblation to cease, and for the overspreading of abominations he shall make *it* desolate, even until the consummation, and that determined shall be poured upon the desolate (Daniel 9:27).

⁵ And I stood upon the sand of the sea, and saw a beast rise up out of the sea, having seven heads and ten horns, and upon his horns ten crowns, and upon his heads the name of blasphemy. 17: And that no man might buy or sell, save he that had the mark, or the name of the beast, or the number of his name. 18: Here is wisdom. Let him that hath understanding count the number of the beast: for it is the number of a man; and his number *is* Six hundred threescore *and* six (Revelation 13:1, 17-18).

⁶ After this I beheld, and, lo, a great multitude, which no man could number, of all nations, and kindreds, and people, and tongues, stood before the throne, and before the Lamb, clothed with white robes, and palms in their hands (Revelation 7:9).

Chapter Seventeen: The Rapture & Tribulation

[7] And I saw heaven opened, and behold a white horse; and he that sat upon him *was* called Faithful and True, and in righteousness he doth judge and make war. 14: And the armies *which were* in heaven followed him upon white horses, clothed in fine linen, white and clean. 16: And he hath on *his* vesture and on his thigh a name written, KING OF KINGS, AND LORD OF LORDS (Revelation 19:11, 14, 16).

[8] For we wrestle not against flesh and blood, but against principalities, against powers, against the rulers of the darkness of this world, against spiritual wickedness in high places (Ephesians 6:12)

[9] And when the thousand years are expired, Satan shall be loosed out of his prison, 8: And shall go out to deceive the nations which are in the four quarters of the earth, Gog and Magog, to gather them together to battle: the number of whom *is* as the sand of the sea. 9: And they went up on the breadth of the earth, and compassed the camp of the saints about, and the beloved city: and fire came down from God out of heaven, and devoured them (Revelation 20:7-9).

[10] And white robes were given unto every one of them; and it was said unto them, **that they should rest yet for a little season**, until their fellowservants also and their brethren, that should be killed as they were, should be fulfilled. 20:4: And I saw thrones, and they sat upon them, and judgment was given unto them: and *I saw* the souls of them that were beheaded for the witness of Jesus, and for the word of God, and which had not worshipped the beast, neither his image, neither had received *his* mark upon their foreheads, or in their hands; and they lived and reigned with Christ a thousand years. 20: 5: But the rest of the dead lived not again until the thousand years were finished. This *is* the first resurrection (Revelation 6:11; 20:4-5).

[11] Heaven and earth shall pass away: but my words shall not pass away (Mark 13:31).

Understanding the Scriptures

[12] But I say unto you, That every idle word that men shall speak, they shall give account thereof in the day of judgment (Matthew 12:36).

[13] And whosoever was not found written in the book of life was cast into the lake of fire (Revelation 20:15).

[14] Ye therefore, beloved, seeing ye know *these things* before, beware lest ye also, being led away with the error of the wicked, fall from your own stedfastness (2nd Peter 3:17).

[15] And I saw a new heaven and a new earth: for the first heaven and the first earth were passed away; and there was no more sea. 2: And I John saw the holy city, new Jerusalem, coming down from God out of heaven, prepared as a bride adorned for her husband (Revelation 21:1-2).

Appendices

Appendix One: The Nine Gifts of the Spirit

1. **The word of wisdom:** The ability to give advice, understand and explain various issues in the Bible. For instance, if you have a meeting with someone who starts asking the complicated questions about the Godhead, God will give you words of wisdom when responding, thus avoiding confusion.

2. **The word of knowledge:** Knowledge is something that is obtained in the natural realm; however, there is also spiritual knowledge, which in the Bible is referred to as the word of knowledge. The word of knowledge knows things about specific situations that only God Himself can reveal. For instance, when Paul rebuked the woman with the spirit of divination in *Acts 16*. Paul was able to discern the spirit because he had the gift of knowledge; thus he knew the truth about this woman. The same can be said about Peter when he rebuked Ananias and Sapphira in *Acts 5*.

3. **The gift of faith:** According to the Bible every man is given a measure of faith (*Romans 12:3*). Also, the Bible says that if a person has faith the size of a mustard seed

that they can speak to a mountain *"be removed"* and it will happen (*Matthew 17:20*). Everyone has faith and faith is at work even when we do not realize it. The gift of faith is a higher dimension of the measure of faith and mustard seed faith. Individuals that have this gift can speak and what they speak will come to pass. For instance, there was a man who had no food, and he asked his wife to boil some water and told his family to sit down to the table because they were about to eat. He then told them there were going to bless the food that they were about to receive. As soon as he finished praying someone started knocking at the door. To his surprise, it was some church members with food. This indeed was the gift of faith at work.

4. **The gift of healing:** The person with this gift specializes in praying for those who are sick. It is important to note that if either person does not believe there will be no healing.
5. **The working of miracles**: This is similar to the gift of healing; however, the working of miracles has many avenues whereas the gift of healing only has one avenue.
6. **The gift of prophecy:** This is merely revealing God's

mind for the future, and it must conform with the Word of God.

7. **Discerning of spirits:** As mentioned Paul discerned the spirit in the women in *Acts 16*. The Bible notes that the woman had a spirit of divination. She called Paul a man of God which was a fact, but this grieved Paul, and he rebuked her because he discerned an evil spirit at work. This gift recognizes merely the presence of an evil spirit either in someone or in the atmosphere. As children of God, we need to realize that there are evil spirits in people and the atmosphere. When aware of this, we need to use the power of God within us to rebuke the evil spirits in the name of Jesus. However, if we live a prayer less life or are not full of the Holy Ghost, we are powerless, and the devil will not be cast out.

8. **Divers kinds of tongues:** There are three purposes for tongues. Firstly, for personal prayers. Secondly, it is an indication that one has obeyed the gospel plan. Thirdly, it is used for the edification of the church. This gift can be used in any one of these areas.

9. **Interpretation of tongues:** This is explained in the Word of the Lord. *1st Corinthians 14* notes that when a

person prays in tongues, he is praying unto God and that no one understands. However, if prophesying (giving an interpretation) people should understand because this edifies the church. Those who talk in tongues are edifying themselves, but those that interpret edify the church. Interpretation of tongues is to be done in an orderly fashion. First, there should be two or three people at the most that can talk in tongues. Afterward, one person is to interpret the message. Once again this gift is used to help, rebuke or encourage the church.

Appendices

Appendix Two: The Tribulation

The Seals (Revelation 6, 8:1),

1. The antichrist will win the world to himself. This can only happen when he is revealed. Consequently, this seal has yet to be opened contrary to some beliefs.
2. There will be no peace and people will kill each other. This is happening at the moment, however during the tribulation, *"...brother shall betray the brother to death, and the father the son; and children shall rise up against their parents, and shall cause them to be put to death" (Mark 13:12).*
3. There will be worldwide famine, which has yet to happen.
4. One-fourth of the world's population will die via violence, hunger, etc. This has yet to happen if it did it would have been broadcasted on the internet, television, etc. This seal debunks the theory that tribulation has started.
5. Persecution of the saints. At present, some people are persecuted for the gospel sake. During the tribulation, many will not follow the antichrist. The antichrist will kill these people, and the Bible declares that they will receive white robes and that they will rest for a season. This is not the church as mentioned in the final chapter of this book.

6. There will be an earthquake that will cause darkness, a lunar eclipse and the stars from heaven will fall. All of this will cause people to go into hiding. Recently I saw a documentary regarding the apocalypse, and numerous people have built secret hiding places to avoid judgment.
7. There will be silence in heaven for 30 min.

The Trumpets (Revelation 8, 9)

1. Hailstones containing fire and blood will destroy one-third of the green space.
2. A meteor will destroy one-third of everything in the sea, one-third of ships and one-third of the water will turn into blood.
3. A meteor will cause one-third of the water to become poisonous which in turn will cause death.
4. Darkness upon the earth.
5. A meteor will hit the earth causing darkness, and God will send locusts for five months to sting the men of the earth who took the mark of the beast.
6. A two hundred thousand man army will kill one-third of the population.
7. A worship period in heaven. This is not the last trumpet as some claim nor is it referencing the Rapture *(Revelation*

11:15).

The Vials (Revelation 16)

1. Sores will afflict those with the mark of the beast.
2. Everything in the ocean will die.
3. Water will turn into blood.
4. The sun will burn hotter than usual thus scorching many.
5. Darkness and great pain will come upon the earth.
6. The river Euphrates will dry up for the battle of Armageddon.
7. The seventh vile causes lightning, thunder, the greatest earthquake ever will happen at this point, and 100-pound hailstones will destroy whole cities.

References

Bernard, D. (1985). *Practical Holiness: A Second Look.* Hazelwood Mo: Word Aflame Press.

Bacchiocchi, S (1997). *Christian Dress and Adornment.* Biblical USA: Perspectives Publishing.

Camara, B. (2006). Men's Short Haircuts and the Barber Shop. Retrieved from, http://www.ftmguide.org/haircuts.html

Carmela, M. (2005). *History of Wedding Rings.* Retrieved from, www.amalfi-wedding-planner.com/eng/StoriaFedi.htm

Gentles, I. (1995). *Euthanasia and Assisted Suicide: The Current Debate.* Canada: Stoddart Publishing.

Harris, J. (2003). *Sex is not the Problem Lust is.* USA: Multnomah Publishers Inc.

Minois, G. (1995). *History of Suicide: Voluntary Death in Western Culture.* Baltimore and London: Johns Hopkins University Press.

Pack, D. (2008). *The Truth Behind St. Valentine's Day.* Retrieved from, http://www.thercg.org/articles/ttbsvd.html

Pack, D. (2002). "Trick?" or "Treat?" Unmasking Halloween Retrieved from, http://www.thercg.org/articles/totuh.html

Pack, D. (2008). The True Origin of Christmas. Retrieved from, http://www.thercg.org/books/ttooc.html

References

Pack, D. (2008). The Truth Hidden Behind Makeup. Retrieved from, http://www.thercg.org/books/tthbm.html

Peck, M.S. (1997). *Denial of the Soul: Spiritual and Medical Perspectives on Euthanasia and Mortality.* New York: Harmony Books Publishing.

Reynolds, R. (1987). *Old Testament History.* Hood River: Alpha Bible Publications.

Got Questions Ministries. (2002-2017). What Is the Christian view of human cloning Retrieved from, https://www.gotquestions.org/cloning-Christian.html

Other Publications

Have you ever wondered what lust is all about? Lust is full of deceit, envy, jealousy, and wickedness. Lust attacks almost everywhere you go. You never seem to find a place where lust is not found. Lust has a way of keeping people's minds very busy, no time to relax. It has a way of making people feel powerless. Overcoming at times  may seem impossible, but this book teaches you how to overcome lust. This book is not filled with religious jargons; rather, it offers plain talk from the heart of one of God's servants who has experienced the onslaught of lust. This book will help you in your quest for victory.

Visit www.ltapostolic.org to order copies of this book and to contact the author.

About the Author

Stephen Hogan was born to Isabel Turley Hogan and the late Harold Raymond Hogan in 1981. At the age of two, his father died, and it was left to his mother to raise him. When it came time for Stephen to start school throughout his years in elementary, he struggled academically due to the loss of his father.

At the age of twelve Stephen was sent to a specialized school to help him succeed; however, Stephen made friends with people who were negative influences. However, God's hand was upon his life, and at the age of thirteen (1994) Stephen was baptized in Jesus name and received the Holy Ghost. From that point forward he was faithful to the work of the Lord.

In 1999 Stephen dropped out of high school due to his academic struggles. It was also in 1999 when he had a vision from the Lord and was called to preach the gospel. His passion for reaching people and for succeeding from that moment on grew daily.

In 2001, Stephen returned to adult education and completed his high school studies in June of 2004. In September of 2004, he enrolled in Special Care Counseling and completed his D.E.C at Vanier College. Stephen has worked with children, youth and seniors, and with each experience, his desire to help people grows deeper and deeper.

In 2005, Stephen enrolled in the Québec Pentecostal Bible College and completed the two-year program to obtain his first ministerial certificate. In 2010, Stephen returned to Bible college (Purpose Institute) and completed four additional years of study to earn two more ministerial degrees (diploma of associate in ministerial studies and bachelors in ministerial studies). During this time he also went on various missions trips and helped establish churches.

On January 1, 2011, Stephen was instructed by the Lord to start Lighthouse Tabernacle Apostolic. After three years of evangelizing on January 7, 2014, the ministry was granted the official documents from the Québec government, which recognized Lighthouse Tabernacle Apostolic as an official ministry. On August 30, 2014, the ministry was officially blessed, and Pastor Hogan was formally ordained as a pastor.

Pastor Stephen Hogan is a true man of God. God has called him to a particular ministry. His unique gift for reaching out to people is just one of the many qualities that God has used to build his ministry. His devotion to the work of God reflects his willingness to respond to God's call. His passion and desire are to teach the Word of God and to share the love of God with people.

www.ingramcontent.com/pod-product-compliance
Lightning Source LLC
LaVergne TN
LVHW011357080426
835511LV00005B/324